The Rent Trap

Also available

Being Red
A Politics for the Future
Ken Livingstone

Syriza
Inside the Labyrinth
Kevin Ovenden
Foreword by Paul Mason

Cut Out
Living Without Welfare
Jeremy Seabrook

The Rent Trap

How We Fell Into It and How We Get Out of It

Rosie Walker and Samir Jeraj

PlutoPress
www.plutobooks.com

First published 2016 by Pluto Press
345 Archway Road, London N6 5AA

www.plutobooks.com

The Left Book Club, founded in 2014, company number 9338285 pays
homage to the original Left Book Club founded by Victor Gollancz in 1936.

British Library Cataloguing in Publication Data
A catalogue record for this book is available from the British Library

ISBN   978 0 7453 3646 6   Paperback
ISBN   978 1 7837 1749 1   PDF eBook
ISBN   978 1 7837 1751 4   Kindle eBook
ISBN   978 1 7837 1750 7   EPUB eBook

This book is printed on paper suitable for recycling and made from fully
managed and sustained forest sources. Logging, pulping and manufacturing
processes are expected to conform to the environmental standards of the
country of origin.

Typeset by Stanford DTP Services, Northampton, England

Simultaneously printed in the European Union and United States of America

Contents

Series Preface

The first Left Book Club (1936–48) had 57,000 members, had distributed 2 million books, and had formed 1,200 workplace and local groups by the time it peaked in 1939. LBC members were active throughout the labour and radical movement at the time, and the Club became an educational mass movement, remodelling British public opinion and contributing substantially to the Labour landslide of 1945 and the construction of the welfare state.

Publisher Victor Gollancz, the driving force, saw the LBC as a movement against poverty, fascism, and the growing threat of war. He aimed to resist the tide of austerity and appeasement, and to present radical ideas for progressive social change in the interests of working people. The Club was about enlightenment, empowerment, and collective organisation.

The world today faces a crisis on the scale of the 1930s. Capitalism is trapped in a long-term crisis. Financialisation and austerity are shrinking demand, deepening the depression, and widening social inequalities. The social fabric is being torn apart. International relations are increasingly tense and militarised. War threatens on several fronts, while fascist and racist organisations are gaining ground across much of Europe. Global warming threatens the planet and the whole of humanity with climate catastrophe. Workplace organisation has been weakened, and social democratic parties have been hollowed out by acceptance of pro-market dogma. Society has become more atomised, and mainstream politics suffers an acute democratic deficit.

Yet the last decade has seen historically unprecedented levels of participation in street protest, implying a mass audience for radical alternatives. But socialist ideas are no longer, as in the immediate post-war period, 'in the tea'. One of neoliberalism's achievements has been to undermine ideas of solidarity, collective provision, and public service.

The Left Book Club aspires to meet the ideological challenge posed by the global crisis. Our aim is to offer high-quality books at affordable prices that are carefully selected to address the central issues of the day and to be accessible to a wide general audience. Our list represents the full range of progressive traditions, perspectives, and ideas. We hope the books will be used as the basis of reading circles, discussion groups, and other educational and cultural activities relevant to developing, sharing, and disseminating ideas for radical change in the interests of the common people at home and abroad.

The Left Book Club collective

Acknowledgements

We appreciate the generosity of everyone who agreed to be interviewed for this book, especially those who have the most to gain from renting remaining as it is. Thank you.

Thanks to Emily Wraith, Heather McRobie and Tansy Hoskins for sage advice on publishing. Thanks to Caroline Walker for arduous transcribing and eagle-eye editing, and to Charlie Tims for clear thinking and immense tolerance.

CHAPTER ONE

The Rent Trap

Rosie Walker

Corinne fishes in a cardboard box for some cups, boiling water in a pan on the hob because she hasn't yet unpacked her kettle. 'It's annoying that the cooker is different every time you move', she says, fiddling with the controls. She's been in her new south London flat for a week, and likes it. There's a huge cheese plant in the corner of the living room, and a decked balcony that she's looking forward to sunbathing on.

She had been dreading telling her son that they were moving again. He celebrated his seventh birthday in the last few days at the old flat, and – to Corinne's surprise – did not object to packing up his presents as soon as he had opened them. This is their fourth home in five years. 'In the end, he took it well', says Corinne. 'I was surprised at how mature he was about it.'

Corinne (not her real name) is 33, with a well-paid job in policy for a campaigning charity. She has a good university degree, specialist skills, and is articulate and smart. But buying a home of any kind is out of the question, for good. Hers is no horror story: there have been no cockroaches, no dodgy wiring fixed with Sellotape by letting agents, no beds in sheds, no landlords with baseball bats. She is not on the run from violence or debt or the courts. She is simply a private renter in 2015, and her story is an everyday one.

Her son could have found out about the house move by accident, when a woman from a well-known high street letting agent tried to let herself into their home without permission, to take photographs.

Corinne had been paying £1,150 per month, excluding bills, for a two-bedroom flat in south London near to her job – an amount that used up most of her salary. 'It was nice; we stayed for two years', Corinne says, in a way that makes two years sound like a lifetime. After two years, the landlord demanded an extra £100 a month, though no improvements had been made to the flat. Corinne could not afford it, and negotiated the increase down to an extra £25 per month. Her landlord owns 90 flats in London and Kent.

Shortly afterwards, the letting agent who for legal reasons we shall call Denfields (not its real name) telephoned to ask if they could come and take photos. Corinne contacted her own letting agent to ask what was going on. 'They said "haven't you got the letter? Your landlord's putting the rent up to £1,300, effective from next month." But I hadn't been told anything', says Corinne.

Corinne went away for a week, trying to ignore daily emails and phone calls from Denfields, saying they wanted to go to her flat and take photos. When she returned, she called them and asked what they wanted to take photos for. '"I live here!" I said. "I haven't said I'm moving out!"' She called her own letting agent who said they didn't know. 'Then, within an hour, they'd emailed me a Section 21, and told me that a rent increase of £125 per month applied to the two-month notice period.'

Corinne contacted Renters' Rights London, who explained that rent cannot legally be increased in this way. But Section 21, the part of the 1988 Housing Act that allows a landlord to evict with two months' notice and without having to give a reason, cannot, in most cases, be legally challenged. For Corinne, it was devastating. 'The landlord had total disregard for his tenants. And to try to make me pay an extra £250 at the end, when he was the one making me move out and leave the community my son goes to school in – I was furious.'

Denfields kept up the bombardment of calls, demanding to be let in to take photos, but Corinne was busy at work. They even emailed to accuse her of changing the locks – a legal right that tenants have, but that Corinne had not used. It was then that she realised they had been trying to get in without her permission. Tenants must give explicit permission for anyone – even the landlord or agent – to enter their home, even if they have keys, but the agents from Denfields seemed unaware of this law and emailed Corinne's landlord to say that Corinne was 'not co-operating'.

Corinne's son had had a difficult term at school, but had eventually settled. She didn't want to tell him the news until she had secured a new home, so she could say for certain whether or not he would have to move schools, and she knew that agents coming to take photos of his home without explanation would unsettle him. 'I didn't want him lying in bed at night worrying about all the possibilities, and where we might end up', she says. Besides, she didn't want her 'whole life on show' online.

When she explained this to her landlord, adding that she had no legal obligation to pay any extra rent without a new tenancy agreement, he replied that if she 'co-operated', she wouldn't have to pay the £250. 'I felt that was like saying "You've got less money than me, so I'm sure you've got lower levels of integrity", Corinne says. 'As if I were only pretending to care, and that it could easily be remedied with £250 – which was mine anyway.'

Knowing that Denfields had tried to get in without her permission changed everything. 'After that I wanted to get out all the sooner, because I'd stopped feeling comfortable there. I started double locking the door, putting the chain on when I was at home. It's not that I thought my life was threatened or anything, it's just that I didn't feel safe in my home in the way that I used to. I didn't know who else the agent might have given keys to.'

Corinne grabbed every spare moment she could to look for a new home without her son noticing. After getting advice, she emailed the tenancy relations department at Southwark Council, asking them to carry out their legal duty to protect her from harassment – even if that just meant emailing the landlord and agent to explain the law. 'The council guy backed up what Shelter and Renters' Rights London were saying, but when I asked him to put my rights in writing he seemed annoyed because he didn't want to have to type an email. It took him four working days to reply, which is a long time when you're dealing with an urgent situation', Corinne says.

Nevertheless, Southwark Council's tenancy relations officer eventually did his job, and emailed the landlord and both sets of agents to explain the law: that Corinne had no obligation to pay increased rent for the final two months as nothing had been agreed, and that no one could enter Corinne's home without her permission. Simply giving twenty-four hours notice is not sufficient, regardless of what any tenancy agreement says, since a contract cannot trump the law. He warned the landlord and Denfields to seek legal advice before entering. Corinne shows me all the emails, including one from the landlord threatening to 'implement' the unauthorised rent increase for the final two months because she was not being 'co-operative'.

Denfields ignored the legal advice from Southwark Council and responded by emailing Corinne, simply stating that she would be coming to let herself into her flat the following week. Southwark Council's tenancy relations officer told Corinne to instruct a solicitor to take out an injunction against Denfields and recommended a local solicitor, who said they would charge £2,000 plus VAT – which Corinne could not afford to pay. All she could do was email Denfields again, reiterating that she did not give her consent for them to enter her home.

Until this point, it had appeared as if the Denfields employee had only misunderstood the law. But when she emailed Corinne's landlord, it became clear that she understood it perfectly: she just didn't respect it. Corinne shows me the email chain, which her current agent had accidentally copied her into in the flurry. Minutes after Corinne reiterated that she did not give her consent for anyone to enter her home, the Denfields employee wrote to Corinne's landlord to say that Corinne was 'not playing ball' and to warn him that Corinne had dared to speak to a public authority.

'I feel like she is going to do everything in her power to prevent us coming over', the Denfields employee wrote. 'I feel she is going to escalate this if we enter the property without her consent. She really isn't playing ball. By law I can't go over if she says I am not allowed. She has copied in the council too.'

At the last minute, Corinne's frantic search for a new home – carried out at night while her son was asleep, or in lunch breaks at work – paid off, and she found a flat she could move into within a week, extending her bank overdraft by £3,500 to cover the first month's rent and the deposit. After their barrage of threatening emails, Denfields and the landlord backed down and made no further attempts to enter the flat while Corinne was living in it.[1]

Sitting in the new flat, surrounded by half-unpacked boxes showing colourful rugs and children's toys, I ask Corinne – whose work involves speaking to women and girls about sexual consent – whether she sees any parallels between that and the way the landlord and his agents had tried to manipulate her into questioning her rights. 'I'd not made the connection before, but yes', she says: 'They *assumed* my agreement; that's not consent. They make you feel as if you're some sort of disagreeable harpy: 'you said you'd do this, you're not doing this, it's my property'. It's that trick of turning it around and making themselves the victim of something, when actually you're the one paying them all this money. The way they turn it on its head – that's what makes people not want to speak out. Because you worry about how you'll be perceived by other people. They made an agreement that the flat would be mine, for an agreed fee. But they don't get that they can't have it both ways: you can't take practically the entirety of someone's pay, every month, and then still want the flat to be yours.'

At 33, Corinne has never missed a rent payment or not paid a bill. She has never caused damage – accidental or deliberate – to any home. Yet the simple act of researching her legal rights and contacting an official – in this case, a tenancy relations officer at her local council, whose job is to inform the borough's private landlords about the law – marked her out to the landlord and to Denfields as a 'problem' tenant. Though she had done nothing wrong, Corinne feared her new landlord would ask her old one for a reference, and, since such references are unregulated and can be based purely on how much a landlord likes or dislikes someone, that simply standing up to bullying could have made her homeless. In the event, they did not ask.

As renting stories go, Corinne's is average, but Corinne is not. Most private renters do not get as far as researching their legal rights, assuming, instead, that what they are told by their landlord or high street letting agent must be true. Others are too consumed coping with the demands of life – work, childcare, relationships, health – to find the time or energy to put up a fight. Some are so dismayed to discover how few enforceable rights private renters actually have that they just shrug and move on. After all, if you can be 'asked to leave' your home for no reason, and if rent can be set at any amount during times of housing shortage, what use is knowing what to do about a broken shower?

Corinne's new landlord is a housing association. Once charitable trusts providing only social housing, housing associations have recently 'diversified', seeing the financial gain there is to be made from the private rental market, which now houses 11 million people in the UK. Unlike a social tenancy, which would offer lifelong or long-term tenure, this contract is a twelve-month assured shorthold tenancy (the standard private tenancy), but Corinne is optimistic. She hopes that despite her limited legal status as a private renter, a housing association will be less likely to sell up, to issue a no-fault eviction or to increase the rent.

'If I can just get my son into that school round the corner then at least we can live in the same home until secondary school', she says, going quiet at the thought of the next four years. 'It's not quite what I can afford, but I'd rather pay this and feel a bit more secure than pay a bit less and end up having to move again. Moving costs so much money.' She adds that when she gets her deposit back from her last place, she can pay off the money she borrowed for the current one, and then she'll 'chip away' at the rest by budgeting carefully and selling her possessions on eBay. Like most of London's 2.5 million private renters, she needs to live where the work is.

The most recent English Housing Survey, an annual government survey of 13,300 households, found two thirds of private renters had been living in their home for less than three years, and a third had been resident for less than a year.[2] With homeownership out of reach for anyone on an ordinary salary, and social housing accessible only through waiting lists that are decades long, a quarter of all families with dependent children now live in the private rented sector. A 2014 Shelter survey asked 976 private renters with dependent children, all of whom had moved home in the last five years, about their experience. Fourteen per cent had had to change their child's school, and 13 per cent said the house move had been upsetting or stressful for the child.[3]

This is not a problem for private renters in most developed countries, where the right to stay – if you have done nothing wrong – is either indefinite (for example, in Germany, the Netherlands, Denmark, Sweden and Switzerland) or between three and five years (in Ireland, Spain, France, Austria and Norway). In a 2011 international comparison from LSE, which compared private rented sectors in 16 developed countries, only Australia equalled the UK in having a legal minimum of six months. Even in the US, the minimum is one year.[4] Housing campaign groups including Shelter have long argued that longer tenancies are the easiest way to give renters enforceable rights, reduce neighbourhood 'churn' and protect families and relationships, but the landlord lobby has fiercely resisted, knowing that this would mean landlords losing a degree of power over their tenants.

In defence of the short-term tenancy, landlords argue that many tenancies happen to run on for longer than the legal minimum, quoting research from the National Landlords Association (NLA) that finds the average tenancy lasts for 2.3 years. They hope, perhaps, that policy makers will not notice that the legal right to end another person's tenancy remains in place whether it is used or not. What someone *happens* to receive and what someone is *guaranteed* to receive are different things: most dog owners are not cruel to their dogs, but we still have laws prohibiting dog owners from cruelty. The Residential Landlords Association (RLA), in a recent briefing on tenancy lengths, proposed its own solution: after the standard six or twelve month tenancy ends, the tenant could begin another six or twelve month one, if the landlord chooses to allow it.[5] They fail to point out the obvious: that this is simply a description of what we already have. Who they hope will be fooled by this is unclear. The landlord lobby is explored in more detail in Chapter 7.

But muddying the waters sometimes works. When Ed Miliband put a three-year minimum tenancy into Labour's 2015 manifesto (the Greens chose five years, while the Lib Dems' 'family friendly tenancies' failed to specify a length of tenure), landlords, wary of the growing renter vote, warned renters of being 'locked in' to three-year commitments. In fact, the policy was proposing nothing of the sort: it simply protected renters from no-fault eviction for three years, allowing them to leave, with notice, if they wanted to – in much the same way as you might cancel a subscription to a service you no longer need. Despite being a politician's fudge (Labour's proposal included a preliminary six-month 'trial' period, which could have allowed landlords to end the tenancy there without justification), it was described by the landlord lobby as 'unequal and unfair'. But it was, for the first time in mainstream politics since renting was deregulated in 1988, an acknowledgement that losing a home has a bigger impact on a renter's life than losing a source of income has on a landlord. Few people would recognise the relationship between landlord and tenant as an equal marriage.

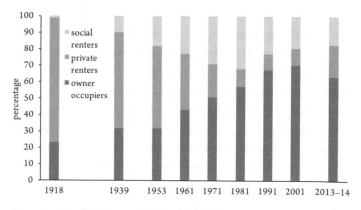

Figure 1   Trends in Tenure, 1980 to 2013–14

Sources: 1981 to 1991: DOE Labour Force Survey Housing; 1992 to 2008: ONS Labour Force Survey; 2008–9 onwards: English Housing Survey, full household example

The majority – 63 per cent – of households in the UK live in homes that they own, either outright or with a mortgage. But the picture is changing rapidly. Private renters now represent 19 per cent of households, while 17 per cent are social renters. Figure 1 shows the subtle but important shifts that occurred in 2012. Of the four groups, private renters have the lowest legal status. When a private renter loses their home, it is not headline news; there's no dramatised public battle like the recent campaigns staged by Focus E15, the group of council tenants in Newham protesting against being rehoused away from London, or the tenants of New Era, whose charity owners sold their houses to a private property company. These protests captured the public imagination precisely because they were defending what private renters have never had: the right to a permanent home.

It was easy to identify with what those protesters were fighting *for*: a family, a neighbourhood, a sense of belonging. But to the untrained eye, it was less obvious what they were fighting *against:* becoming private renters. They knew that would mean searching for a new home every year or two, finding either unaffordable rents or landlords who won't accept the state payments they need to be able to pay those rents. They knew that – even with the kindest landlord and the most agreeable home – the possibility of having to pack up and leave is only ever two months away. For private renters leaving their home – because the rent has gone up, because the landlord refuses to fix the boiler, because the strangers they had to share it with became too difficult – there are no struggles fronted by Russell Brand, and no TV crews. There's nothing to struggle for, nothing to defend. It's an everyday event.

The worst kind of injustice is the kind that is so ordinary, so mundane, that it goes unnoticed by perpetrators and victims alike. Corinne's story is banal; at first glance, there's nothing remarkable about an email exchange with a letting agent who doesn't care about the law, or who describes a tenant as 'not playing ball' when she exercises her legal rights. When private renters complain about another house move, another withheld deposit, another uninvited visit, it almost sounds like whingeing. There's no merry band of protesters pitched against the state or a giant property developer; no obvious David or Goliath.

Corinne made a huge effort to defend the few rights she did have. Most, as the email from Denfields suggests, wouldn't have tried – thinking, perhaps, that it was not worth the time and energy, or worrying that they would appear unreasonable. When private renters seek legal advice, the most common response is embarrassment at believing they had more legal protection than they actually have. Like so many renters' stories, Corinne's has no real triumph, no tragedy, no happy ending. It ends in a state of perpetual insecurity, with few checks or safeguards, and there is little she can do to challenge it. She cannot leave, break away or climb out. There is no exit. We should call it what it is. A trap.

This book is about The Rent Trap. About the economic and political forces that made it possible, the institutions that sustain it, and the culture, inheritance and social mores that have made us all part of it. It starts with policy, and it ends in our attitudes and language. It is a curious tale of buy-to-let mortgages, friends who profit from friends, obscure pieces of legislation, activists who dangle from balconies, and a well-funded but outdated lobby of landlord associations. In the future we might look back on The Rent Trap as a historical quirk. But first we have to see it. It's time to throw open the curtains.

If the rail isn't broken, that is.

CHAPTER TWO

No Rights

Rosie Walker

In October 2013, the BBC news programme *Inside Out* ran an exposé of letting agents in London. Posing as a landlord seeking agents to let his Kensington flat, a reporter canvassed a range of letting agents, saying that he wanted no 'Afro Caribbean' tenants. Ten separate agents reassured him, unaware that they were being filmed with a hidden camera, that they would filter out any black applicants by not returning their calls or telling them that any property they asked about had already been taken.[1]

Viewers were shocked, but they shouldn't have been. Though it had been 45 years since laws against racial discrimination in housing came into force, discrimination on almost any grounds – whether race, gender, class or family structure – goes largely undetected in the private rented sector. It is almost impossible to prove, because a landlord is not obliged to give a reason for selecting one tenant over another, and legal redress is limited. With access to homeownership and social housing blocked, private renters have no choice but to compete with each other for a roof over their head, trying to win the favour of a private individual, who, with a bit of discretion, is at liberty to exercise any prejudice they might harbour – be it outright racism, a preference for a particular gender or sexuality, or simply a dislike of renters who know their rights.

Getting in

Nathan, an agent at Stow Brothers letting agents in Walthamstow, London, organises 'open viewings' to whittle down prospective tenants. He tells me about a recent viewing for what he describes as a 'glorified one-bedroom flat' at £1,350 per month. 'The point was to find the right person', he says, explaining that he and his colleagues considered 'how tenants interacted with us, and how they behaved at the viewing'. He stresses that nobody was encouraged to bid on the rent, though this is known to happen at other rental viewings. He adds that his agency does not take holding deposits (usually a portion of the full deposit that the prospective tenant gives the agent to stop them showing it to other clients) until the landlord has accepted a tenant's application.

After the viewing, Nathan received seven applications, which he narrowed down to three before putting the finalists before the landlord. A couple with children were instantly ruled out. 'It's definitely a personal thing, who the landlord likes', he says, adding that his letting agency encourages landlords to meet prospective tenants in order to 'build trust'. I ask if I can talk to one of the landlords Nathan's agency works for, about what characteristics they're looking for in a tenant. 'I can tell you', he replies. 'Landlords are looking for people that are like themselves.' Like themselves in what way, I ask. The same race? The same class? The same sexuality? 'That they're earning enough money to be able to afford the rent, and do all the normal things they would do in their everyday life. Basically being nice, decent normal people', he says, adding that he's organising another open viewing for a different flat nearby, where the landlords have said they don't want 'multiple sharers' because they think it would mean extra 'wear and tear'. Wouldn't the landlord be able to rule out flat sharers from the application, I ask? 'No, not necessarily', he says. 'Some agents would be dishonest about it. Some agents actually rent the properties themselves then let out the rooms and collect the difference in rent. All kinds of things they shouldn't be doing.'

Private renters searching for a home frequently find adverts that say 'No DSS', meaning people who are eligible for housing benefit payments to cover all or part of their rent (the Department for Social Security, or DSS, has not existed since 2001, but the term has somehow stuck). Landlords say this preference is due to the unreliability of councils who administer the payments, arguing that administrative errors lead to late rent payments. Others argue that the preference is based on ignorance and prejudice, pointing to derogatory comments made in online forums used by less-educated landlords.

What many fail to realise is just how many of the UK's 11 million private renters rely on housing benefit to cover their rent. Since 2010, the number of private renters receiving housing benefit has stayed well above 1.25 million, reaching 1.46 million in 2013.[2] Many of these are in full-time work, but rents have risen while earnings have not. This leaves even those with relatively well-paid jobs needing state help to meet the demands of their landlords. A single person over 35 years old without children, for example, earning £30,000 a year and renting a one-bedroom flat in Hackney, is eligible for around £110 per month in housing benefit as part payment towards the rent.[3]

With fewer landlords willing to accept tenants on housing benefit and more people needing it, some letting agents have spotted a gap in the market. Aki Ellahi, a letting agent in Wolverhampton, says 475 of the 500 homes that his agency manages are open to people on housing benefit. He has also set up DSS Move, an online portal allowing renters to search a national database of homes, though he admits there are few available in high demand areas like London. 'If you get it right, it can be a good market to rent to', he says.

Every renter who registers with his agency must set up an account with the local credit union, which transfers the tenant's housing benefit payment to the letting agency as soon as it comes in, but, unlike a high street bank with a direct debit to fulfil, the credit union does not allow the tenant's account to go overdrawn if the benefit payment is late.

The biggest complication for renters employed on zero hours contracts is that their housing benefit must be recalculated each month according to how many hours they have worked – so Ellahi takes care of the admin for them. But his is no social service. 'It's in our interests to ensure that we collect housing benefit from the tenant', he says. 'If we can't, our business won't survive.'

London borough councils, who have a legal duty to house people who have become homeless in their borough, like what Ellahi does. 'We get sent five or ten tenants from London every week', Ellahi says. 'London councils will phone us and say "We've got someone we need to house but there's nowhere cheap enough in London, so if we pay you some money, can you house them?"'

The amount councils are willing to pay as a one-off fee varies, but Ellahi says it's 'around £3,000' per tenancy. Does this not make it tempting, from a business point of view, to shunt tenants out each year to make way for new arrivals from London? 'No', he says, 'we're more people oriented than that. And we've usually got around ten empty properties that people can move into', adding that tenants on full housing benefit tend to stay for several years. Prospective tenants sent by London councils have the right to turn down a home they don't like, but in some cases doing so will strike them off the council's list: there's a complicated set of criteria they have to meet if they are to be allowed to hold on for a social tenancy or a home in another area.[4]

Ellahi learned his trade from his parents, and knows the people and authorities in his local area well. He speaks about his tenants respectfully. But given the increasingly precarious nature of work and the ever-upward rise of unregulated private rents, does it make sense to treat 'the DSS market' as distinct? Wouldn't it be wiser to dispel the myths about benefits instead, and prevent letting agents from discriminating unfairly? 'I don't think you ever will', Ellahi says. 'Because it's a tricky market and letting agents are lazy people. They just want someone who neatly ticks all the boxes. Most letting agents don't know their palm from their wrist.'

Staying in

Once a tenancy has begun, the problems are far from over. Standards are difficult to enforce because much of the enforcement duty falls to under-resourced local authorities who see their funding cut each year. The criminal courts are inadequate when it comes to dealing with the behaviour of landlords and letting agents; the civil courts offer penalties that could be a genuine deterrent but there are limited opportunities to use them, and court costs are a barrier. Organised crime in private renting is rife, particularly in London. And, while Section 21 of the 1988 Housing Act allows a landlord to evict a renter for any reason or none, any rights that a renter might have on paper – the right to have something repaired, for example – are woefully undermined.

Tessa Shepperson, a former housing solicitor, runs a legal information service for landlords. Landlords and letting agents can ask for legal advice online, either paying a fee to get an instant answer or waiting to have it answered on the blog for free. Landlords who pay a membership fee can attend conferences and workshops to learn more about housing law, though, like any landlord organisation, those who choose to do so usually represent the more conscientious end of the spectrum. Landlords who prefer to ignore the law are unlikely to join.

Despite this, Tessa encounters a surprising level of ignorance. The most common query, she says, is from landlords who want to evict a tenant but discover that they can't because they haven't put the tenant's deposit in a recognised protection scheme (discussed further in Chapter 5). Another sticking point is getting landlords to understand that they don't have the right to enter their tenant's home without the tenant's permission. The confusion comes, she says, from clauses in most tenancy agreements that say a landlord must have access to carry out repairs, and that giving 24 hours notice is enough. But a tenant's 'right to quiet enjoyment' of their home – a statutory right dating back to 1925 and established in case law in 1986 – overrides anything written in a contract.

'Lots of landlords just don't get it', says Tessa. 'They think "it's my property". But a tenancy is still a type of ownership. They don't realise they have effectively sold it for a fixed period of time.' Of course, any renter who chooses to exercise this right may well find themselves receiving a no-fault eviction notice.

Tenants are not often in a position where they can take their landlords to court, Shepperson says, partly because they're more likely to be intimidated by the legal process than a landlord is, but mostly because of prohibitive court fees (a claim for an unprotected deposit, for example, could incur fees of up to £1,000). And compensation for disrepair is far harder to win than a landlord bringing a case against a tenant for unpaid rent. 'I wrote an online guide for tenants on how to bring a claim for an unprotected deposit', says Tessa, 'but I ended up taking it down because I was so worried about the fees that tenants would have to pay. It's typical of the government, isn't it? They introduce this right, and then they put it into a system that makes it very difficult to implement.'

Local authorities have long struggled to keep tabs on what private landlords are up to in their borough. Though councils have a duty to intervene where there are poor housing conditions in a privately rented home, when a private landlord harasses a tenant or when a local letting agent breaks the rules, many councils struggle to devote adequate resources to the problem and some choose a more laissez-faire approach. Typically, a London borough council will have less than five tenancy relations officers (TROs) to deal with 30 to 40 thousand privately rented homes, with similar numbers of staff in trading standards and environmental health departments. Even those who want to rein in the power of private landlords are afraid to do so, as local private landlords are often a council's last resort when trying to house the homeless – though, of course, this comes at a high price.

The 2004 Housing Act gave councils a new tool, but made it hard to use. They could make it mandatory for all private landlords in the borough to apply for a licence, costing them around £100 per year (£8.50 per month) and requiring them to meet basic standards. The rub was that no extra money was available to carry out inspections or enforce penalties – apart from in the east London borough of Newham, where a central government grant of £1 million allowed Newham to become the first borough to set up a mandatory licensing scheme, which they did in January 2013.[5]

Landlord licensing can't tackle everything – there's no mechanism to control rent levels, for example – but for the first time, it requires landlords to declare who they are and what they are doing, making them visible to the taxman as well as to local authorities. Landlords have fought hard against licensing plans in any borough considering such a scheme, threatening to increase rents as an expression of their indignation. The National Landlords Association (NLA) organises local groups of landlords to lobby any council considering a licensing scheme, with some success: in December 2014, one landlord in Enfield, north London, personally funded a judicial review against the council and partially won on the basis that the council hadn't consulted residents in neighbouring boroughs. This caused other councils, fearing the cost of a judicial review, to tread with more caution.

Though the number of landlords and agents available to take part in council consultations vastly outweighs the number of renters able to do so (the consultation in Newham in 2012, for example, found 110 landlords and agents willing to take part in the council's discussion forum, and only 12 private renters), landlords have also employed other tactics, such as attempts to dub licensing schemes a 'tenant tax' and issuing warnings that renters will face unlimited and unannounced inspections. The landlord lobby is discussed in more detail in Chapter 5.

Richard Tacagni, who worked in local authority housing and environmental health for twenty-two years, now runs London Property Licensing, a consultancy service for landlords and agents who want to know more about the new requirements. 'Most people aren't even aware of the licensing schemes that do exist', he says. 'So lots of landlords haven't applied for a license, and there's not a huge amount of enforcement.'

Each council running a licensing scheme makes its own decisions about how to handle it, so some are more effective than others, he explains. A fundamental flaw in the design of the scheme is that the money made from the licensing fee can only be used for its administration, rather than for enforcement, though the Housing and Planning Bill currently going through Parliament could change this. He also thinks that stronger enforcement of other rules, such as one that came into force in 2014 requiring all letting agents to register with an official redress scheme or face an instant £5,000 fine, could serve the same purpose as licensing without the administrative burden. This, however, is another rule that many councils are choosing to ignore.

But the real power of licensing lies in its ability to switch prosecutions from the criminal to the civil courts. Ben Reeve Lewis, who spent 25 years working as a tenancy relations officer for Lewisham Council in south London, says the criminal courts do little to deter bad landlords, while the civil courts hit them where it hurts the most: the wallet. He compares two recent prosecutions for illegal eviction: one case, against Oxford landlord Johnson-Bowler, was tried in the criminal court in 2011. The landlord was sentenced to 60 hours community service, with £100 compensation for the tenant and £500 in court costs. The other, an almost identical case against the agency Best Move Estates, was heard in the civil court – and won £10,624 for the tenant. Criminal proceedings must be initiated by the council, and can mean one staff member from a small tenancy relations team working on the case for a year – making them unavailable for other work – while civil proceedings can be brought far more easily.[6]

'I once had a case where a landlord threatened a tenant and her three children with a gun', Reeve Lewis says. 'It took two and a half years to get him to court and he was fined £400 – and the court refused to cover our court costs, which were about £8,000 by that point. But if we had licensing, I know of loads of landlords like him that we could pull the plug on overnight.'

Between the 1990s and 2008, Reeve Lewis says, the work of a tenancy relations officer focused on preventing illegal evictions – often involving violent landlords who were helped by police ignorant of housing law – and illegal private lettings of council flats by council tenants who could sell their keys on the black market for £8,000. But everything changed around 2008, he says:

> Around 2008, there were four big shifts. First, amateur landlords were ushered in as people looking for an alternative pension – who didn't understand the game at all – flooded the market with rental properties. Trivial to middling complaints started coming in, and the landlords were breaking laws they simply didn't realise were there. Then there were the reluctant landlords. They were like the

amateurs, but their reason for being a landlord was that they couldn't sell their house.

Then there was an explosion in letting agents. In Lewisham in the early 1990s, there were 30 or 40 agents in the whole borough. By 2015 there were well over 150; unscrupulous chancers entering an unregulated market looking for a fast buck without the slightest bit of experience or knowledge.

But without a doubt, the biggest game changer of the last 25 years in private renting in London has been large-scale, organised crime. There's so much money to be made from property now – and it hasn't escaped the attention of money launderers, drug dealers and people traffickers.

Councils are 'hopelessly outgunned' in the current climate, he says. 'The powers they've got only work if the target offender is genuinely concerned about prosecution, and if the enforcement teams can make legal sense of all the aliases and fake companies designed to throw them off the scent.'

Jamie Finn, a private renter in Edinburgh, took his landlord to court in 2013 after he threatened to shoot him and tried to kick his door down. His landlord, Mark Fortune, had let himself into Finn's rented home without permission, to show another tenant around. Finn and his flatmate took the opportunity to ask him about repairs that were long overdue: a broken washing machine, a broken shower, a broken window.

'He literally went from zero to explosion', Finn says, adding that Fortune boasted about having three friends who had been in prison for shooting someone, and threatened to 'kick the f***' out of him and his flatmates. But they were quick witted enough to record the explosion on a phone. Fortune left and the tenants had time to lock the door before he came back and tried to kick it down.

Neither the local council nor the police offered any help. 'When we called the police and gave them the recording, initially they said he was *allowed* to kick in the door', Finn says. Finn found other tenants of the same landlord, and eventually their case was taken on by the Scottish public prosecutor. The case was complicated and drawn out, hindered by the fact that Finn had been too frightened to turn up to the initial court hearing. In the run up to the hearing, Finn repeatedly received threatening phone calls from Fortune. Fortune was convicted of a breach of the peace – not harassment – and fined just £650. He was also removed from Edinburgh's landlord register, which operates in a similar way to a licensing scheme, but Finn fears that it will be easy for Fortune to keep the property and register it under a different name.

Getting out

Landlords can evict tenants legally without reason, by serving a Section 21 notice which lasts for two months. After the two months has expired, the landlord must then get a court order giving the tenant a date to move out. There are a few restrictions on the use of Section 21: it cannot be served if the council has issued an improvement notice for serious disrepair, or if the landlord has failed to protect the tenant's deposit, or if there is no gas safety certificate. Many renters not au fait with the intricacies of housing law will leave anyway; some will not even realise this counts as an eviction, and there is no official body that records no-fault evictions.

Some landlords prefer to use other techniques to get their tenant out sooner. Legal methods include imposing an unaffordable rent increase or letting things go unrepaired in the hope that the tenant will move out 'voluntarily'. Intimidation and harassment (including changing the locks, removing a tenant's possessions, and threatening or using physical violence) are illegal, but often used.[7] The lines are blurred by specialist eviction companies, such as Landlord Action, who will undertake 'eviction work' for a fee. As their website boasts: 'There are invalid notices served every week, but nobody ever knows because the tenants leave. That's fine.'[8]

In 2012, Sheffield landlord Jay Allen received a nine-month prison sentence for using violence to illegally evict a tenant. It was the first time in 20 years that a prosecution brought by a council had led to a prison sentence. The jury heard that Allen had recruited a friend to physically remove the tenant, who was in rent arrears, from his home. When the tenant, Chris Blades, told his landlord he was breaking the law, Allen replied: 'Do I look like I care?' The judge, reported the *Sheffield Star*, said Allen had intended to 'dominate, frighten and overwhelm'.[9]

Local authorities have had the power to prosecute private landlords and their agents for harassment and illegal eviction since 1977. But the Protection from Eviction Act, passed to counter the types of landlordism associated with the infamous Peter Rachman (discussed in Chapter 6), is rarely used by councils who simply do not have the resources to pursue every case they hear about. 'It wasn't unusual to get three in one day, though that wasn't regular', says Reeve Lewis of his time as a tenancy relations officer (TRO) for Lewisham Council: 'If you say "ok, I'm going to take this case", you were off the ball for a week, taking statements, gathering evidence, serving summonses, etc. There were only two TROs in my borough and 35,000 private renters. If we got an illegal eviction on Monday, then by Friday we could have four or five, and if I was taken off the ball dealing with the first one, I couldn't do the others – so they didn't get justice. One day, I had a guy who had come back from holiday and couldn't get into his house. So he went to the letting agent to ask what had happened and they said "Ok, come into the back room to chat about it", so he did, and they punched him in the face and threatened him with a gun. When he reported it to the police, the police refused to deal with it.'

Renters experiencing harassment or illegal eviction, since they are criminal offences, should call the police. But police forces have a poor record in dealing with these situations. According to Giles Peaker, housing solicitor and editor of the Nearly Legal housing law blog, many police mistakenly believe it is a civil matter and turn their backs, while a few actively help the landlord remove the tenant. 'The general experience of most housing advisers and housing lawyers is that the police are next to useless', he says. 'Unless there is someone out there training the police, they are fairly ignorant.'

Cases brought against the police for assisting in an illegal eviction are rare, but not unheard of. One, in November 2009, saw Greater Manchester Police settling the case out of court by paying the tenant £2,500.[10] Councils are currently free to choose whether or not to prosecute for harassment and illegal eviction, usually having to base their decision on the resources available. Dave Hickling, chair of the Association of Tenancy Relations Officers (ATRO) thinks prosecution should be made a statutory duty, though how to fund that remains a thorny question. When the government's Communities and Local Government Select Committee conducted an inquiry into private renting in 2013, some argued for this measure but were disappointed that the committee failed to include it in its recommendations. 'We see no justification for a postcode lottery where landlords are able to get away with harassment and illegal eviction in some areas but not in others', Hickling says.

Freedom of Information (FOI) requests made for this book show there were only 443 prosecutions for illegal eviction in England and Wales in nine years between 2003 and 2012, and only 226 of these ended in a conviction. As long as a landlord has the right paperwork, a legal eviction is relatively easy and a no-fault or Section 21 eviction cannot be challenged in court. But some progressive lawyers have begun to look for new solutions. Dirghayu Patel, a solicitor at GT Stewart Solicitors, says the 1998 Human Rights Act offers one solution: Article 8 sets out the 'right to respect for private and family life, home and correspondence', and adds 'there shall be no interference by a public authority with the exercise of this right'. 'We're still very much in the early days', says Patel, 'but the courts have begun to look at whether the court, as a public body, can try to strike a fair balance between landlords and tenants.'

A 2014 case, *McDonald* v. *McDonald*, examined a tenancy between relatives in which the private landlord had gone bankrupt and used a Section 21 to evict their tenant. The Court of Appeal ruled that Article 8 of the Human Rights Act cannot be applied to private individuals, but this has been appealed in the Supreme Court and many lawyers eagerly await the outcome this year. So far, the Supreme Court has accepted that Article 8 does apply to social tenancies, where the landlord is a council or housing association. Because these bodies are considered part of the state, they can only evict as a last resort when alternatives to eviction have been exhausted. But it's only the state that has a duty not to breach a person's human rights, not an individual. The only way around this is to argue that the court is part of the state. 'It could be quite groundbreaking', says Patel.

Article 8 has already been used with some success. Patel describes a recent case of retaliatory eviction in Peterborough. A tenant had asked his private landlord – who happened to be the Church of England – to tackle the disrepair in his home. The landlord issued a Section 21 eviction notice instead, and Patel filed a human rights defence on the basis of the disrepair. 'The landlord got their chequebook out and paid the tenant £10,000 plus court costs', says Patel. The tenant chose to take the money and drop the case.

Few know about the uses of Article 8, Patel says, because not all cases are reported in the law books. The lower courts – county and magistrates courts – hear a large proportion of eviction cases, where transcripts are not always produced, and some clients do not want details published even when their solicitor has been successful. So far, it has not been successful in preventing an eviction of a private renter because in most cases the landlord chooses to pay off the tenant. And few renters will get this far due to lack of legal advice. Cuts to Legal Aid in 2013, and patchy advice provision from councils, have made things worse. Even the best informed tenant will still, in most cases, face prohibitive legal fees.

'Since the 1988 Housing Act there's been a whole generation of tenants that have not been able to exercise the rights they do have', says Patel, adding that the rules on deposit protection that were part of the 2004 Housing Act were drafted so badly that they have had to be amended twice since then, and that he wonders whether this was by design or default. 'People are very ignorant, and maybe it suits the government that they are that way.'

CHAPTER THREE

No Money

Samir Jeraj

It's Saturday morning on Brixton High Street in South London. Campaigners and local residents have gathered outside the tube station. Georgie, a local musician, tells me that the number of evictions from privately rented homes has risen in this area, whether directly – through Section 21 notices – or indirectly, by sudden and unaffordable rent hikes. One group here, Save Cressingham Gardens, campaigns against the demolition of social housing in Lambeth, and another, Save Guinness AST, is here to support some small businesses threatened by rent rises in the nearby railway arches.

The group set up their banners, one reading 'Social Housing Not Social Cleansing', outside Foxtons the letting agent. Georgie walks straight into the branch, sits on the edge of a chair, wriggles into a sleeping bag and lies on the floor. The staff look nonplussed, lock the door to stop anyone else entering the shop, and retreat to the back room. After 15 minutes or so, the police arrive and Georgie is encouraged to lie down in front of the shop instead. The police are in no mood to arrest anyone – not least because none of the Foxtons staff had asked Georgie to leave. After walking out, he tells me one of the police officers told him the cost of housing meant he now had to commute to Lambeth from Bedford.

Private renting has become more expensive, while wages have stagnated and benefits have been cut, leaving private renters caught in the middle. Confusingly, indexes that measure rents vary widely, and even government researchers are unsure of the best way to measure them. Industry indexes, produced mostly by letting agents, want to show rents rising as high as possible in order to attract custom from landlords, while landlords themselves want to downplay rents to counter the threat of rent controls and regulation from policy makers.

To give an idea of just how confusing this can be, the estate agents Countrywide reported at the start of 2014 that average rents (based on an index of 50,000 homes) had risen to £854 a month. Only a few months later, LSL Property Services claimed the average rent (based on their index of 20,000 homes) was £753 a month.[1] In June the same year, the Office of National Statistics (ONS) stated the national median rent was in fact £595 across all rented homes in England and £1,300 across rented homes in London.[2] Unlike commercial indexes, which use asked-for rents in online adverts,[3] the ONS records the rents actually paid using data from the Valuations Office, who collect data on half a million rents.[4]

But seeing rent rises of anywhere between 2 and 10 per cent reported at the same time leads to widespread confusion. To compare rents from one year to the next, the data needs to be 'mix adjusted', meaning the sample must have the same 'mix' of one-bedroom, two-bedroom and three-bedroom homes. It should also be adjusted to account for regional variations.[5]

The Joseph Rowntree Foundation estimates that, without intervention, by 2040 rents will rise by 90 per cent above inflation. A 2015 report from the National Housing Federation revealed that, as a proportion of their earnings, UK renters pay double the rent of their European counterparts.[6] So while it is clear that rents are increasing, the actual amount paid is difficult to pin down – and this is partly because there is no national register of landlords, which could require them to declare their rental income. There are significant regional variations, too – many of which go beyond the obvious distinctions between the capital and the rest of the country. A 2015 report from letting agents Homelet showed that while overall costs remain highest in London, the rate of increase is actually faster in areas outside of London. The south-west, for example, saw one of the biggest rent rises between 2014 and 2015.[7]

'What comes in goes straight out again'

In spring 2015 CJ Hole, a letting agent in Bristol, posted letters to prospective clients asking, 'are you getting enough rent?' This is a common practice in areas of high demand and some households receive several each week. The letter continued, 'with rents increasing every week in Bristol, it is highly likely that your property is due a rent increase'.[8] It boasted that CJ Hole had recently let out a one-bedroom flat for £835 a month and a two-bedroom house for £1,500. While most renters who receive these notices put them straight in the recycling bin, local residents in Bristol started an online petition denouncing 'predatory rental practices', which gathered 11,000 signatures.[9]

Paying high rent makes it hard to save money; paying rent that uses most of your disposable income makes it impossible. Government data show two-thirds of renters have less than £1,500 in savings.[10] Renters with children have, on average, only £63 a month to put into savings. Breaking that down a bit further, the vast majority of privately renting families cannot save more than £50 a month and more than half of renting families are not able to save at all. To put this in context, the average deposit in 2015 for a mortgage was £71,078.[11] This means the average privately renting family would take 94 years to save up for the average deposit on a home: perhaps longer than any of them will live.

Thea is 29 and lives with her husband and their two children in a ground-floor flat an hour from central London, paying £1,000 a month in rent excluding bills. This is half of their household income. They moved there after their rent in a more centrally located but unfashionable area was raised beyond their means. But the threat that it will happen again hangs over them.

'What comes in is what comes out', Thea says, adding that they try to save, but would never be able to save enough to buy a home. 'We are living in fear that our landlord is going to raise our rent this summer.' Thea's children go to local children's clubs, and moving would disrupt them. Since they moved further out of London, the family have found it harder to attend their church in central London which now takes almost an hour to reach. The constant moving also makes it hard to form the social ties that many parents rely on. 'It's difficult to find babysitters or have people come round.' And, like most private renters, Thea says she daren't ask for repairs or home improvements for fear that her landlord will impose a rent increase in response.

Thea's husband is a teacher, and some places on shared-ownership schemes are reserved for people like him (definitions of 'key worker' are loose and vary significantly, but usually include teachers, nurses, doctors, police officers and other public sector workers on what is often called the 'front line'). She and her husband applied to one scheme, but their application was turned down because the monthly mortgage payments would have used 43 per cent of their household income, a proportion considered by shared-ownership schemes to be too high. But they already spend 56 per cent of their monthly household income on rent.

'I don't feel that there are many options out there for us', Thea says.

Fees, forms and frenzies

Letting agent fees are an ever increasing cost for private renters, and are not scrutinised in the same way as rent is or reflected in official statistics. Helped by the growth of buy-to-let mortgages, whose holders tend to pass their properties on to letting agents, letting agents are free to charge fees to the tenant for anything they choose, whether that be signing a form, photocopying it, issuing the tenant with a key or, sometimes, even an 'admin fee' to cover the cost of charging all the other fees. The only limitation, introduced in May 2015, is that agents must display all fees up front before a renter signs a contract. Failing to do so is now punishable with a £5,000 fine from the local council, but many councils prefer to turn a blind eye.

Renters usually start by seeing an advert for a home (or, in areas of high demand like London, a room in a shared flat). Even at this stage, renters are vulnerable. One well-known 'scam' means anyone with a mobile phone or an email address can pose as a letting agent, show prospective tenants around an empty flat they have broken into, and then collect holding deposits and signing fees before 'disappearing' and doing it again under a new name. While this is obviously illegal, local authorities lack the resources to police it adequately.

Once a renter has chosen a home, letting agents will refer them to a credit referencing agency, which will recommend whether they should be allowed to rent it based on their income and credit history. Those who are self-employed, on fixed-term job contracts, or in any other increasingly common precarious situation, must offer a guarantor – usually a relative who owns property – or several months rent up front. Letting agents can then charge an extra fee of around £50 for a 'guarantor check'. Some agents bypass this system altogether by asking prospective tenants to 'secure' their tenancy by paying an up-front reservation fee – but there is no obligation for agents to honour this.

A year before the new rules were introduced in 2015, Coventry Citizens Advice Bureau researched the fees and practices of 97 letting agents. They found private renters were being charged up to £1,500, including the rental deposit and a month's rent up front, to begin a new private tenancy. Only one in four letting agents posted their fees on their website, and more than half would not disclose their fees when contacted. In one case, five students paid a total £1,500 reservation fee to hold their house over the summer, but the letting agent didn't keep their side of the agreement.[12]

In Scotland, agency fees have been unlawful since 1984, but it was only in 2012 that the law was clarified and enforced. Letting agent umbrella bodies claim this has led to higher rents,[13] but a 2013 report from Shelter showed that rents were no more likely to rise in Scotland than in England, where agency fees remain legal. The report found that only 1 per cent of landlords had seen a rise in fees charged to them by their agents, and they had passed this cost on to tenants. Among the letting agents surveyed, 59 per cent said the ban on fees had had no impact on them, 24 per cent said it had a negative impact, and 17 per cent actually said it had a positive impact. More than half said the clarification in the law had had a positive effect on private renting.[14]

But while fees are banned in Scotland, many letting agents still charge them, and many private renters, unaware of the law, still pay them. Between May and July 2012, more than 800 private renters sought help from Shelter Scotland to reclaim more than £100,000 in illegally charged fees.[15] A year later, an investigation on BBC Radio 5 revealed that agents across the UK were regularly breaking the law on fees, and that the 20 biggest councils in the UK had prosecuted a total of only 12 cases in 2012 between them.[16]

Alyson MacDonald from the Edinburgh Private Tenants Action Group (EPTAG) says many agents get around the Scottish law by charging a higher first month's rent instead of fees, and when a renter does try to challenge their fees in court, landlords and letting agents drag the case out to increase stress and financial costs for the renter in the hope that they will drop the case. 'They kept phoning him up to persuade him to take less money and settle out of court', she says of one EPTAG member who pursued their case recently, adding that most private renters cannot afford the legal support available to letting agents and landlords.

In the past, a rental deposit was the equivalent of a month's rent. But in the last few years, six weeks' rent has become more common – and those without guarantors or permanent job contracts can be asked for a year's rent up front. A Kent Citizens' Advice Bureau reported in 2014 that one prospective tenant with a poor credit record had been charged £650 for a credit check, £1,150 for a security deposit, and was required to pay six months' rent up front. Six months later, when it was time to renew the tenancy, the agent demanded 12 months up front. Taking rent in advance is also a common way for landlords to avoid having to put a deposit into a protection scheme.[17]

Rent control in other countries

A poll by Survation in early 2015 found that a majority of the UK population, including a majority of homeowners and Conservative voters, favoured intervention to lower rents.[18] Even centre-right think-tank Civitas has embraced the idea of rent controls and said that Labour's plan for capping rent increases within a three-year tenancy was 'not enough'.[19]

Most European countries, as well as some cities in the US, have laws to control overall rents or restrict rent rises in certain areas. In New York, landlords can increase rents for tenancies that began after 1971 by a maximum of 7.5 per cent every two years. Paris rents are capped at 20 per cent above the market average and must be based on the size, age and location of the home – a policy introduced by President Hollande after rents in the city had been shown to have risen by more than 40 per cent in ten years.[20] Germany has a central government index that records rents charged on all types of housing, taking into account the location of the home, the condition it is in and what local amenities are on hand. Renters can challenge any rents that are a certain percentage above the averages recorded in the index by applying to the criminal courts, and local authorities determine what that percentage should be.

In 2015, Berlin set it at 10 per cent of the local average and extended the policy to all new private tenancies in the city.[21]

In the Netherlands, rents are set by a points system based on the size, condition and features of the home. During the first six months of their tenancy, a renter can challenge their rent by going to the local rent commission. These rules apply to three quarters of privately rented homes.[22] In Switzerland, any rent increase must be justified by the landlord, who must demonstrate to a court that the home has been improved or that the expense of letting it has increased. In Denmark, where rent controls apply to nine in ten privately rented homes, local authorities choose which model of rent control to use: one system bases maximum rents on the running costs faced by the landlord, with an allowance for maintenance and a fixed profit margin.[23] Venezuela sets a maximum rent based on 3 to 5 per cent (per year) of the cost of building the property, and local committees that include renters adjudicate individual cases.[24]

Daniel Bentley, a researcher for the think-tank Civitas, is an unlikely advocate of rent controls. 'I know it may seem unusual for a pro-market think-tank to be calling for regulation, but the housing market is failing', he says. The private rental market in the UK is 'crowding out' both social housing and owner-occupation, he says. 'They tend to buy the stock we've already got, then rent it to people who can't afford to buy that stock.' Bentley says that both the Labour Party and campaign groups like Shelter fail to take a long-term view of private renting, and he thinks that the landlord lobby exerts a 'worrying' level of influence on UK housing policy.

The solution, he says, is three-fold: first, we must ask how big we really want the private rented sector to be, and at whose expense its growth should come. Second, renters need rent controls and more secure tenancies. Third, we should encourage institutional investment in private renting, shifting the ownership from unaccountable private individuals to accountable companies. Institutions, like pensions funds, are less interested in rising house prices and would rather have long-term predictable income from stable rent, Bentley says.

Most of the opposition to rent control is based on the view that in the twentieth century it led to a shrinking of the number of privately rented homes, but, Bentley says, it was actually the rise of social housing, and of building societies in the 1920s and '30s, that meant fewer people needed to rent privately. 'There is a lot of myth about what rent controls did to this country', he says.

Though he is cautious about comparing the UK to Germany, Bentley sees the latter as a good example of a healthy, functioning private rental market. But, he notes, Germany does not have an overall shortage of housing because it has maintained a high rate of new building. In exchange for government subsidies to build, private landlords signed up to rent controls and security of tenure. As a result, there is little need in Germany for social housing – which Bentley thinks the UK should retain. 'We've got a system which is geared less and less to what people want in housing, and subjecting it to the whims of people who have got the money to buy homes at inflated prices', he says.

Little research has been done into how rent controls might work in a modern setting in the UK. Research from Cambridge University in 2015 (commissioned separately by Shelter and the London Assembly Housing Committee) took six different rent control models and, using these as hypothetical scenarios, asked landlords how they would react to each. The six models were:

1 Limiting rent increases to inflation rates in a new five-year tenancy.
2 Limiting rent increases on new tenancies to inflation rates or average wage rises (whichever is lowest).
3 A three-year freeze on private rents followed by a return to market rents after the three-year period is over.
4 Limiting rent increases to inflation rates or average wage rises (whichever is lowest), but exempting new-build housing and housing that has become privately rented for the first time.
5 Cutting rents to two thirds of their current level, then limiting increases to inflation or average wage rises (whichever is lowest).
6 Setting rents above market rates, but granting an automatic 29-month extension to a six-month probationary tenancy, which could only be ended by the landlord if the tenant is at fault or if the landlord genuinely wants to move into the house themselves.

728 private landlords and 97 letting agents responded to an online survey, and 20 (as well as eight buy-to-let mortgage lenders) were interviewed in depth about how they might respond to each scenario. Unsurprisingly, private landlords said they would object to most of these measures, and some said they would sell their properties as a result.[25]

In the researchers' own words, conclusions are 'tentative': what people say they will do is different from what they will actually do. Landlords who say they would respond to rent controls by letting their properties sit empty, for example, are effectively saying that receiving no rent is better than receiving some rent. This would need to be seen to be believed.

The study concluded that five of the six scenarios would help to stabilise rent levels and could have a small impact on the growth of the number of privately rented homes. Scenario five (cutting rents by a third then limiting increases to inflation or wage growth), is the exception: this could decrease rents significantly, and landlords said that in this scenario they would either sell, or let their properties sit empty.

Mindful of their lobbying position under a Conservative government, Shelter used the research to justify their choice not to advocate for rent controls.[26] But Stephen Knight, a Liberal Democrat member of the London Assembly Housing Committee is more critical: 'The argument suggests that the only things that are "viable" are things that will make no difference to affordability. And if you're not going to make a difference to affordability, then what on earth is the point? It's a "rent control model" that doesn't frighten the landlords. Well, if it doesn't frighten the landlords then it's not worth the paper it's written on. The whole point of rent stabilisation is to frighten off a few landlords. We need them to take their money somewhere else – somewhere where it won't have such a damaging effect.'

A common assumption is that discouraging investment from private landlords would reduce the supply of privately rented homes. While this argument works when applied to industries that create new products, it works less well when applied to privately rented housing. Private landlords do not, on the whole, build new houses – they buy existing ones, and they could not take those houses with them if they were to leave the market. If they were to sell their properties, more homes would be available for first-time buyers or for landlords better able to cope with a smaller profit margin, house prices could gradually decline, and fewer people would be stuck in the rent trap. No amount of economic modelling can accurately predict every outcome, and it is far from clear how many landlords would actually sell their properties and what effect this would have on house prices.

Knight says policy makers should be bolder in standing up to financial interests. 'If anything that will make a difference to affordability ends up making it unattractive for investors to enter the housing market, well that ought to tell you something about the housing market', he says. 'The investors are the problem. Or at least, they're part of it.'

Fears of a sudden crash are unfounded, Knight says, as landlords would be unlikely to sell simultaneously, and protections could be built in to protect owner-occupiers who have over-mortgaged. 'The idea that we have a sort of nuclear button that would make the whole thing collapse – well, it wouldn't collapse.'

Much of the confusion comes from the number of private landlords who say their main motivation is capital gains, rather than a profit on the monthly rent. They rely on the monthly rent not for an income, but to buy the capital asset for them.

Knight says rent controls alone would not tackle the problem of affordability, and he advocates a higher capital gains tax on buy-to-let owners – who are currently charged 28 per cent capital gains tax if they let their properties sit empty. 'If I had my way I would double that, at least', Knight says. 'At the moment, everybody agrees that house prices are out of control. But no-one's wiling to say that they want to do anything to bring them down.'

Housing benefit: private renting below the poverty line

More than 3 million renters now live in poverty, and the Joseph Rowntree Foundation estimates this number will rise to nearly 6 million in the next 25 years.[27] Analysis from the New Policy Institute (NPI) in 2013 found 4 million of the nation's 11 million private renters are now in poverty, and that well over half of those are in work.[28] The NPI attributes this to welfare reform, low wages and spiralling housing costs.

Private renters who struggle to cover their rent can claim housing benefit to help them survive, and, historically, private landlords with knowledge of how the benefit system works have increased their rents to the maximum amount available in benefit. Data from the Department for Work and Pensions (DWP) shows that housing benefit paid to private landlords was two-fifths of the total housing benefit bill in 2013–4.[29] In that year, private landlords received £9.5 billion of public money.[30] Government research estimates that this figure will rise to £10.8 billion by 2018/19.[31]

Changes to benefit rules in 2010 limited the amount of housing benefit a person can claim, introducing the 'local housing allowance' that pegged the maximum rate at the thirtieth percentile of the local market price. This meant that only three in ten, rather than half, of all privately rented homes in an area would now be affordable for private renters on housing benefit.[32] In 2012, new changes broke the link between market rents and housing benefit altogether: instead of housing benefit rates reflecting changes in local market rents, they now follow Consumer Price Index (CPI) inflation rates. This means that, year on year, rents can rise at a faster rate than housing benefits. The government claimed that reducing housing benefit would reduce rents, but their own analysis in July 2014 showed that rents did not drop and that renters, rather than their landlords, shouldered the costs.[33]

Many private renters find themselves forced to 'top up' the amount they can claim in housing benefit in order to stay in their home: figures in a 2012 study from Crisis, the charity for single homeless people, suggested that almost a million private renters were already doing this, some of them using savings or money that they needed to pay other bills.

In addition to new ways to calculate the maximum amount of housing benefit a renter can claim, the government introduced an overall cap in 2010, set at £250 a week for a one-bedroom home and £400 a week for four-bedroom home. At the time, Crisis estimated that fewer than one in ten homes in central London would be available to people on housing benefit.[34] In anticipation of the cap, councils in London began to move families out of the city: a 2010 survey by BBC London found that 13 of London's 32 councils were already trying to rehouse homeless families in Luton and other more affordable parts of the UK.[35]

Other changes to housing benefit have affected private renters, too. Until 2012, single private renters over the age of 25 could claim enough to cover a self-contained home, if their circumstances dictated it. But in 2012 the age limit shot up to 35, meaning that single private renters under that age who need housing benefit can only claim enough to cover the cost of a room in a shared house – a house that they might have to share with strangers. Crisis said this change would affect more than 60,000 people, and would, for some, halve their housing benefit payment overnight. Though the rules make exceptions for renters with children, the policy disproportionately affects homeless people, ex-offenders, pregnant women and people with mental health problems, Crisis says.[36]

In April 2013, the government limited the total amount of combined benefits a family can receive to £500 a week. Analysis from the New Policy Institute shows that this means all 32 of London's boroughs – even the very cheapest ones – are now off-limits to families with three or more children if no one in the household is in work.[37] Plans to reduce this cap to £400 are on the table.[38]

Out-of-work benefits such as Job Seeker's Allowance have become more conditional, so private renters who find themselves out of work and who fail to meet ever more stringent criteria face a higher risk of rent arrears and eviction. Under the new Universal Credit system, which rolls all benefit payments into one, the housing component can be sanctioned if the DWP rules that a part-time worker is not doing enough to find full-time work.[39] A 2012 Crisis study examined the effects of the 'first wave' of the Coalition government's welfare reforms, and found a third of the people affected were private renters.[40]

CHAPTER FOUR

No Home

Samir Jeraj

In November 2014 I met a young man who lived on my road in north London, in a flat with no cold running water. Unable to persuade their landlord to fix it, the man and his flatmates were using the hot water tap, filtering it, and cooling it in the fridge before drinking. They were paying over £1,000 a month between them for a flat where they had to fight for even the basics like water.

Where we live affects our health: that much is obvious. But sanitation and heating are only the most visible part. Poor conditions, which make renters unwell, but also insecurity and weak rights, undermine our sense of home. While serious repair problems in a privately rented home are a matter for the overstretched local council, less serious problems – a faulty shower, for example, or a broken piece of furniture – are often left untackled. Local advice centres are inundated with complaints about poor conditions. When Coventry Citizens Advice Bureau compiled research on local letting agents, they linked poor agent practices to low housing standards: private landlords who pay agents a 'management fee' assume the agent will deal with repairs, while agents argue they have no 'incentive' to do so. One case study in the Coventry CAB's 2014 report read: 'When we first viewed the house, everything seemed to be in working order and in decent condition.

However, when we moved in there were numerous problems that [had been] hidden: a downstairs shower that was almost unusable, with a broken holder that we had to replace at our own expense; a leaking roof; pipes under the upstairs bath in poor condition and held in by bricks; the poor condition of upstairs pipework meant that using the shower/bath wasn't possible without causing damage to the downstairs ceiling; smashed garage windows; broken door steps and patio tiles; and broken and unreliable heating.'

In 2000, New Labour introduced the 'Decent Homes Standard', setting out for the first time a tangible set of criteria that all public housing should meet. It was never intended to apply to privately rented homes, but a Shelter report found that by 2014, while 15 per cent of socially rented homes were still failing to meet the standard, a third of privately rented homes also fail (as well as 20 per cent of owner-occupied homes).[1]

Environmental health consultant Stephen Battersby says the worst housing conditions have always been found in privately rented homes, and that recent cuts have made it harder for councils to offer private landlords grants or low-cost loans for home improvement. 'The private rented sector has always been a "Cinderella" part of local government', he says, meaning that of all the problems councils deal with, this one never gets to go to the ball. 'And now, just when local government needs to act, they have their resources cut.'

Battersby describes a home he inspected recently that a local council was using to house formerly homeless people. 'The risks were appalling, not necessarily from disrepair, but from layout and fire safety.' The necessary inspections weren't done, he says, because homelessness departments in councils are too quick to discharge homeless people from their caseload, hurrying them into new homes. Once the tenants are housed, he says, they are 'never contacted' if they happen to be outside the borough's boundaries.

Battersby says cold, with its related problems of mould and damp, is the overriding problem in privately rented homes in the UK. The 2013 English Housing Survey found that only 20 per cent of private rented homes are properly insulated – nearly half the proportion in social housing or owner-occupied homes.[2] A 2010 report from the National Centre for Social Research (NatCen) found that cold homes – often too expensive to heat adequately – are linked with common mental disorders such as anxiety and depression, as well as physical health.[3]

Olly Huitson moved out of a house in Greenwich in 2011. 'The radiators looked about 40 years old, and didn't work properly, they only got lukewarm, and some of them didn't work at all.' They asked the landlord to replace them, as the temperatures outside dropped to minus five degrees Celsius in one of the coldest winters in recent years. 'He had the radiators removed and it took a week for the new ones to be fitted.' But, as explained in Chapter 2, many private renters in cold houses find themselves in a 'Catch 22' situation: ask the landlord for improvements such as insulation and risk being evicted, or stay put and make do. Whether the new limits to Section 21 notices (the no-fault eviction notices) can address the problem of cold is a grey area: 'excess cold' is a hazard, but not always a category 1 hazard – which it would need to be before an eviction notice becomes invalid. Chapter 5 describes the evidence produced by Shelter in 2014 showing that one in 12 tenants have chosen not to ask their landlord for repairs for fear of being evicted, and the subsequent changes that were made to legislation in

2015. A separate report from Shelter in 2014 found that 71 per cent of private renters have paid for repairs themselves rather than risk asking their landlords.[4]

Health hazards are not limited to cold. Hattie Grunewald found herself facing a range of hazards when she was a student in Norwich in 2012. Looking back, she describes her landlord as 'the landlord from hell'. After reporting a broken cooker and toilet to him, Hattie and her friends waited months for action, though they were told repairs were 'on their way'. While they waited, kitchen taps and furniture broke. Their letting agent said the landlord was responsible, and that the repairs would be done 'soon', so they waited another six weeks. Eventually, they contacted their student union and the plumbing was fixed – leaving the cooker out of action. Just before the end of term, their landlord paid them a visit, saying he had come to 'examine the damage'. 'It soon became clear that he wasn't here to fix anything', Hattie says. 'He complained about cracks in the linoleum – which had been that way before we arrived – and that we hadn't changed the light bulbs in some of the lights.'

The landlord told them they had committed 'criminal' damage. 'He threatened to evict us all and stormed off, leaving us shaken and upset', Hattie says. 'We were very worried about the state of the house for the rest of the year but afraid to raise further concerns in case we upset the landlord even more. In the end all we wanted to do was get out of the house as quickly as possible and we were only too glad to move.'

Damp and mould pose a particular risk because they are difficult to spot at an initial viewing before a private renter signs up for a home: paint and perfume are sometimes enough to conceal them. Damp and mould are especially bad for children: a 2006 report from Shelter found that cold temperatures and mould increased the risk of physical and mental illness in children. In overcrowded homes, the risk from meningitis is ten times higher than average. Rita Chadha, from the Refugee and Migrant Forum Essex and London (RAMFEL), says even housing rented privately by the Home Office fails to meet health standards.

A 2012 study by the University of Essex looked at the effect of private renting on mental health. Following the lives of 21 people living in privately rented bedsits in Clacton, researchers found the insecurity of the participants' housing contributed to conditions such as depression, and made it difficult for those trying to recover from drug and alcohol problems.[5] In 2015, the campaign group Generation Rent ran a poll asking respondents to self-report mental health problems. Thirty-seven per cent of private renters reported serious anxiety or depression in the past year, compared to 20 per cent of owner-occupiers. Knowing that you can be evicted at short notice without a reason, and that conditions within the home are subject to the arbitrary decisions of landlords and letting agents, allows private renters little control over their lives. Noise, overcrowding, sharing with strangers and the possibility of unexpected rent increases all take their toll, too. Perhaps it's no surprise, then, that the English Housing Survey found in 2013–14 that renters are less satisfied with their lives compared to social tenants or people who own their own homes.

When James Mackenzie moved into a flat in Edinburgh in 2014, his landlord told him he would lose some of his deposit if the furniture was not positioned exactly as it was when he moved in. The third-party adjudication system for deposit claims, introduced in 2007, would have been unlikely to allow a deduction for these reasons, but Mackenzie chose not to take the risk. In another flat in Fife in 1998, his landlord, believing Mackenzie and his housemates were drug dealers, called the police and let them into Mackenzie's home while the tenants were out. The police removed kitchen scales and a large bag of soap powder. In the same home, Mackenzie's landlord prohibited him from letting his pet cats out of the house and criticised his 'city values'. Another landlord refused to let Mackenzie put the electricity bills in his own name, instead collecting the money himself and then denying he had received it. Mackenzie's electricity was subsequently cut off.

Hannah Clare rented a private home as a student in Liverpool in 2013. One day, a handyman walked straight into Hannah's housemate's bedroom; she hadn't even known he was in the house. It transpired that her landlord had let the man into the house using his own key. When Hannah showed him the clause in her tenancy agreement stating that he must give 24 hours' notice (as well as ask permission), the landlord replied that he would 'do as he liked', adding that Hannah must give him 24 hours' notice if she wanted to invite a guest to her home. Later, Hannah and her housemates discovered that the pot of money they kept in the kitchen for shared bills had been emptied. Hannah now lives with her parents. She says that these experiences have made her anxious about renting again, and that living in the south of England where house prices are high means that it is unlikely she will ever be able to move out of her parents' home.

Private renting: a small step away from homelessness

The ending of a private tenancy is now the most common cause of homelessness. The BBC reported in 2014 that the number of people becoming homeless in this way (mostly as a result of a decision by the landlord) had trebled since 2009.[6] While many private renters between tenancies will resort to 'sofa-surfing' – staying temporarily with friends or acquaintances, putting their belongings into rented storage if they can afford it – others face sleeping on the streets. A 2014 Channel 4 documentary reported that one in five young people aged between 16 and 25 had spent time sofa-surfing.[7] Centrepoint, a charity for young homeless people, found that just under half of sofa-surfers spent a month or more in this situation, one in five had nowhere else to go, and just over one in ten was fleeing domestic violence. These are the 'hidden homeless': hidden because they are not yet sleeping on the streets.

At RAMFEL, one day in February 2015, Hussain (not his real name) and his three-year-old son are asking for housing advice. Hussain and his son arrived in the UK from Afghanistan four months ago on a truck. They were immediately found by the police and claimed asylum. For the past two months they have been living in a shared house privately rented by the Home Office from a private landlord. Hussain appears stressed and anxious, and I try to distract his son, who's trying to get his father's attention while he is talking to the advisor via a translator over the phone.

The shared house is crowded: Hussain and his son share a bedroom by the front door. Living with many strangers and being far away from the toilet is causing Hussain's son problems. He cries all the time and frequently wets himself. His father is desperate. The advisor explains that if he complains to the Home Office and attempts to find somewhere more suitable for his child, they could be moved out of London to anywhere in the UK – away from the support network they've managed to develop.

Later that year, I meet a group of refugees from Manchester. One shows me a letter he has received from the Home Office saying he can now stay permanently in the UK. It also gives him four weeks to leave the home in which the Home Office had housed him. It's a stark introduction to housing in their new country.

The lodging house

In Blackpool, eight in ten private renters need housing benefit to cover their rent – an unusually high figure compared to the national average of 35 per cent.[8] Like many seaside towns, Blackpool is a place people go to begin again. Sadly, not every newcomer's life goes according to plan, which is why the city also has the highest number of 'looked after' children. Councillor Gillian Campbell was one of the people who came to start a new life: 16 years ago she left Edinburgh and moved here. She's now the deputy leader of the council and in charge of their work on improving private renting.

She takes me to visit a long-term lodging house run by a woman called Val. Together with two of the local enforcement officers, we sit in the living room and talk about how Val came to be running the home. The house was used for injured solders during the Second World War and she feels the same sense of care for the people who live in it now. The first time she was asked to house a family was in 1982 – until then, the building had been a hotel. Since 1982 Val has provided privately rented rooms to people who would otherwise have nowhere else to go. Back then, the council paid Val a fee for acting as a proxy support worker, taking the tenants to hospital and dentist appointments. This fee was eventually taken away, but Val and her son Nestor continue to play the same role. 'You get used to caring for people and I can't stop', says Val.

The private renters in Val's house are a mix of ages, men and women, and some have been living there for over 20 years. At the moment, a lot of Val and Nestor's new tenants come via the website Spareroom.com. The rooms themselves are basic: a single bed, cupboard, drawers and TV – but Val and Nestor try to find extras where they can. An older lady with incontinence problems lives in one room, and they have installed a private shower. Tony, who has been there for five years, has learning difficulties and mental health problems, but there are in-house social workers and medical staff to ensure he gets his medication.

James, who is one floor up, is another tenant who got on a train one day and arrived in Blackpool, almost by accident, but he keeps to himself the events that brought him here from London. Nestor says James is an educated man, who had been to a top university, but had suffered several crises in his life. James says he finds it difficult to breathe some days, but that he loves the sea air in Blackpool.

This lodging-house is a 'lifeline' for people with nowhere else to go, say housing officers at Blackpool Council. The home created for the residents is down to the attitude of the owners – it is not something protected by law.

From the streets to the rented room

In 2011, the Localism Act gave councils the right to 'discharge' their legal duty to house the homeless by offering them privately rented housing. Previously, applicants had the right to wait for a council home. Since 2011, if they refuse a privately rented home when it is offered to them, they will no longer have the right to be offered other housing. Councils know that privately rented tenancies, usually only 12 months long and with weak legal status, are not the best option for people trying to rebuild their lives. But with a shortage of their own housing, there's no other way for councils to house all those on their waiting lists, and many authorities find that their hands are tied. The cost of homelessness falls on local authorities the hardest. Nationally, in 2014 there were 60,940 people living in 'temporary accommodation' – the halfway house between nothing and a proper tenancy, usually a bed and breakfast or a hostel – and Westminster Council alone spent £41.8 million on temporary accommodation for homeless families in 2013–14.[9]

Not long after the Localism Act came into force, housing charities Crisis and Shelter undertook a research project that followed 100 formerly homeless people (including those who had lived in temporary accommodation and on people's sofas) through the first 19 months of their private tenancy, interviewing them at points along the way. The report, *Sustain*, found half the participants got more coughs and colds, and visited the GP more often, than before they had moved in. People also took longer to recover from illness, if they did at all, because they were unable to address the causes: damp, mould and cold.

Many homes had mould, damp, or infestations, and many parents participating in the study felt that this was causing sleeplessness, bed-wetting or behavioural problems in their children. Hanging over all participants were anxieties about their landlord and whether repairs would be done, rents would be raised, or if they would be evicted at the end of their tenancy. Disabled participants found the layout of the housing impractical, and children had no space to play. When winter came, participants struggled to cover the cost of their heating bills. To make ends meet, some cut back on food. Others heated or lit only one room, or wore layers of clothes and blankets to stay warm. Many of the participants owned no furniture when they moved in, slowly furnishing their homes using loans and help from family and friends. After 19 months, when the study ended, many said they were trapped in a cycle of debt.

Not everyone applying for homeless status gets housed. Families with children take priority, leaving single people at the back of the queue. In 2014, Crisis ran a 'mystery shopping' exercise: actors contacted 16 local authorities posing as single homeless people to test the council's response. Using four different scenarios (someone who has lost their home after losing their job; a young person thrown out of the family home; a victim of domestic violence; a vulnerable person with learning difficulties), the actors made 87 approaches to councils. Fifty of these received what Crisis considered an 'insufficient or inadequate' response – in some cases, no more than a leaflet about private renting. Most of these 50 were in the seven London boroughs visited, where housing of all kinds is in shortest supply.[10]

Homelessness services in councils have seen their budgets cut dramatically. A 2015 report from Homeless Link found that more than two in five councils had cut their homelessness budgets in 2014–15, with the average service being cut by 17 per cent.[11] Steven Barrett, service director at Bristol City

Council, says the rise in homelessness applications is due to private landlords raising their rents and refusing to accept tenants who need housing benefit. In Bristol, the council knows about 41 rough sleepers – the highest the figure has been for five years – and provides temporary accommodation for 359 homeless households. Faced with ever more funding cuts, the council has decided to devote its shrinking resources to preventing homelessness. 'But we are in a city that is one of the most expensive outside of London. House prices are rocketing away, private rents are rocketing away. It's not great', Barrett says.

Where local government fails, charities have to step in. Many charities run 'access schemes' to help homeless people find – and stay in – privately rented homes. Sarah MacFadyen, policy officer at Crisis, says that lack of council resources means private renting has become the only option for single homeless people – and a growing number of families are being rehoused this way too. 'People don't become homeless because they lose their home', she says. 'They become homeless because they can't find another one.'

Rising rents and cuts to housing benefit mean fewer and fewer private landlords are willing to participate in access schemes. Government departments contradict each other when it comes to housing policy, MacFadyen says: 'On the one hand you have got the Department for Communities and Local Government (DCLG) pushing more people into private renting, and on the other hand you have the Department for Work and Pensions (DWP) cutting housing benefit. [Access schemes] are a very effective form of market intervention. It takes a lot of one-to-one support to make it work for that person. But financially it has huge savings for the public purse to get someone into a decent private rented home. The fact that you always know your tenancy can be ended is a real problem for people, and it really does stop people from thinking of where they are living as their home.'

Many councils offer 'deposit bond schemes', providing the deposit needed to start a private tenancy (usually a month's rent) to people who aren't able to raise the money themselves. But a 2015 report from the Zacchaeus 2000 Trust found these schemes are being replaced by 'incentive schemes', which offer private landlords 'sweeteners' in return for accepting a homeless tenant. The report also found that between 2012 and 2015, councils in London spent a total of £18 million on these incentives.[12]

Meanwhile, central government funding for homelessness has been cut: the Homelessness Transition Fund, a three-year fund that helped charities and councils pay for their homelessness services, ended in 2014.[13] In the same year, the Chartered Institute of Housing called for the government to use the Autumn Statement to establish a £100 million fund to support vulnerable private rented tenants who were at risk of homelessness.[14] When published, the 108-page Autumn Statement failed to mention homelessness.

Innovative councils have set up non-profit letting agencies. Some act solely as a matching service between homeless tenants and private landlords willing to take them on. Others compete in the open market alongside commercial letting agents, hoping that they can drive up standards.

Cadwyn, a housing association in Wales, set up CanDo Lettings using housing association funds. CanDo takes homes from private landlords on five-year contracts and rents them to single people and families on a low income – customers who might struggle to be housed by high street letting agents interested only in the highest price. The agency also accepts referrals from the local council, but will only house tenants needing 'low or no support', leaving those with vulnerabilities to be housed by the council. The council, on their part, provides the deposit, agrees to pay the tenant's housing benefit directly to the agency and offers emotional and practical support to the tenant for the first six weeks. CanDo's manager Francesca Cole says that as well as providing homes for private renters who would struggle on the open market, her agency also frees up council homes for those who 'really need it'.

For some councils, 'social letting agency' is merely a new name for the old Registered Social Landlord (RSL) scheme: a bank of private landlords who councils can use to discharge their homelessness duties, rather than a service for all private renters. But the new type – a non-profit rival to high street agents – is growing. In Wales, the Welsh Local Government Association found social letting agencies now manage around 1 per cent of private rented homes in the areas they operate.[15] Ultimately, their survival depends on their ability to attract custom from landlords, offering a better service for a smaller return. And, amid rising rents and cuts to housing benefit, this relies on the moral conscience of the landlord.

CHAPTER FIVE

No More?

Rosie Walker

One Friday afternoon in November 2014, a furious deputy speaker in the House of Commons shouted at Tory MP and private landlord Phillip Davies, ordering him to sit down. Dawn Primarolo, with a handful of other MPs in the chamber and thousands of renters watching online, had been listening to Davies speak for nearly an hour, filibustering the Tenancies Reform Bill out of Parliament by reading out long passages from the Tories' 1987 manifesto and minutes from obscure select committee meetings.

The bill, dubbed the Revenge Evictions Bill, proposed moderate protection against no-fault evictions, in specific circumstances. Far from a radical overhaul of renters' rights, it simply offered the right to stay for six months – rather than the standard two – to renters who had made a complaint about their home, if their local council considered the complaint to be serious enough. Although it was a private members' bill, meaning it had to be heard on a Friday when most MPs are in their constituencies rather than in Parliament to vote, the coalition government had publicly declared its support for it two months earlier – and so had MPs from all parties. Twenty-six thousand people had emailed their MPs via campaign groups 38 Degrees and Shelter, and others had lobbied their MP directly, asking them to rearrange their

Friday plans to vote for the bill. Members of Davies' own party could be seeing wagging their fingers at him in distaste as he and another Tory MP, Christopher Chope, filled the available time with irrelevant statistics from the government's annual English Housing Survey.

By the time the vote was called, only 60 MPs were present to vote. All voted in favour, but 100 MPs are needed to make it count.

Some were surprised that moves to restrict no-fault evictions had come this far. Campaigners had tried many times before, in the Housing Acts of 1996 and 2004, or through legislation not directly related to housing. But each attempt was fiercely resisted by the landlord lobby. With around 100,000 paying members out of around 2.5 million landlords, the landlord lobby is small. But for its size, it has enjoyed remarkable reassurance from Conservative and New Labour governments.

In November 2011, the coalition government launched a public consultation on the Green Deal, a scheme providing loans to make homes more energy efficient, to be launched in 2013. Housing campaigners pushed for revenge eviction protection to be included in the scheme: no-fault eviction notices could be made invalid if energy efficiency steps had not been taken. But at the National Landlords' Association (NLA) conference in Manchester that month, the burning question on everyone's lips was not about energy efficiency. It was about the power to evict, and whether that power was at risk. A senior official from the Department of Communities and Local Government (DCLG) had been invited to speak, and landlords demanded to know whether revenge evictions protection was likely to be part of the Green Deal.

Believing she was speaking to an audience of only landlords (Geoff Fimister, a housing policy specialist who she would have recognised, was sitting behind a pillar), the government spokeswoman assured them, categorically, that there would be no restriction on the power to evict. The consultation was open to the public for a further two months, and policy campaigners, believing that their contributions would be considered, were laboriously submitting evidence to show that renters in substandard homes were most at risk. This did not matter: the decision had already been made. The landlords would be placated.

But a lot can change in three years. By November 2014, renting had shot up the political agenda and for a private members' bill, this one was attracting unusual attention. An internal spat between the Tories and the Lib Dems meant that the bill, tabled by Lib Dem MP Sarah Teather, had not been whipped. But the government's earlier declaration of support had forced several ministers – including the Housing Minister Brandon Lewis – to walk through the lobby and vote in favour of it. 'Looking back, those two MPs [Davies and Chope] did us a massive favour', says Martha Mackenzie, then public affairs officer at Shelter. 'The cross-party support that had been built up generated a lot of goodwill, and when they talked it out, people were genuinely furious. It created a sense that a great thing had almost been agreed on – and that these two idiots had ruined Parliament at its best.'

Whether the blame lay with the two filibustering MPs or the 590 of them who failed to turn up and vote, the bill was not dead. DCLG staff spoke to Shelter immediately afterwards, suggesting that amendments could be added to another bill instead. Shelter's lawyer worked through the night to redraft the amendments, which were added to the Deregulation Bill before Christmas, and passed in March 2015 – despite another last minute attempt by MP Phillip Davies to derail it.

Who are the landlord lobby?

Almost a third of MPs are private landlords, but this alone does not explain why housing policy is the way it is. The easy view is that those 196 MPs act purely to protect their own financial interest, convincing the other two thirds – most of whom own their homes if not the homes of others – that this is the way things should be. Reality is more complicated, and policy is shaped by all kinds of competing forces.

With no requirement to be on any register, it's hard to know how many landlords operate in the UK. Government estimates say 1.5 million, but figures released by HMRC in May 2015 showed 2.1 million taxpayers were declaring rental income for tax purposes – though HMRC suspects many more do not declare.[1]

The landlord lobby, though its members make up less than 2 per cent of all landlords, is well funded. The National Landlords Association (NLA) alone had a turnover of £3.6 million in the last financial year. In relation to other campaign groups this is not huge (Shelter's was £57 million), but it certainly beats the budget of renters' support groups, many of whom struggle to find £40 to hire a meeting room, and of Generation Rent, the national campaign for renters, launched in early 2014 on a budget of £600,000 for three years. Money does not convert instantly into power, but it does help. Like any other commercial lobby, the landlord lobby has plenty to spend on meetings and events in and out of Parliament, on commissioning research, on consulting lawyers and on framing the debate in the media.

Many organisations make up the landlord lobby: The National Landlords Association and its subsidiary company the UK Association of Letting Agents (UKALA), the Residential Landlords Association (RLA), the Association of Residential Letting Agents (ARLA), the British Property Federation (BPF), dozens of smaller organisations, and, of course, individual landlords themselves. Most of these organisations fought against the Tenancies Reform Bill, but some fought harder than others. A surprise addition at the last minute was the Country and Land Association, representing rural landowners, who appeared at DCLG meetings during the run-up to the reading of the bill, seemingly invited by the RLA.

Alan Ward, Chairman of the RLA, has been a landlord for 22 years and owns five rented homes in Manchester. We meet in a pub in north London, after discovering that the first pub we had arranged to meet in has been closed down and occupied by a property guardian company. When I ask him about the two MPs, Davies and Chope, he's defensive. 'It's a legitimate parliamentary technique', he shrugs. Asked if the RLA put them up to it, he's equally evasive. 'Err … they were given RLA briefings on it, as were other MPs. I don't know whether they rang people in the public affairs department. Anyone can ring up The Public Affairs Company. They probably did', he says.

The Public Affairs Company is a private lobbying firm with clients ranging from energy companies and credit referencing companies to UNICEF and the Pet Care Trust. The RLA pays them £15,000 a year to lobby on their behalf, which includes running the All Party Parliamentary Group (APPG) on private renting. APPGs are informal discussion groups, made up of MPs and Lords from all parties (there must be a minimum of ten members each from the governing party and the opposition, but after that, membership is open to any MP or Lord with an interest, apart from ministers). While some are little more than social groups for shared interests (jazz music, for example, or cheese), others are used as a 'way in' to Parliament: a way to get face-to-face meetings with ministers, to hold discussions, to shift the narrative, to forge relationships. The chair of each APPG (in the case of the private renting group, Tory MP Oliver Colville) has a duty to ensure the group remains 'impartial' – and the privilege of deciding what impartial looks like.

In the last few days before the Tenancies Reform Bill, the private renting APPG held a hurried 'inquiry', similar in style to a select committee inquiry but without the formal status or credibility. They tried to discredit the research Shelter had produced as background to the bill – research that used a YouGov poll of around 5,000 renters, asking how many had been evicted after complaining about disrepair and how many did not make complaints about disrepair for fear of being evicted. The data was then weighted against the English Housing Survey for geography, age and household type. This research was invalid, the APPG said, because Shelter is known to represent the interests of tenants and therefore cannot be trusted.

Instead, the APPG argued, the only valid statistics on the number of revenge evictions must come from a last-minute telephone poll conducted by Landlord Action, a private bailiff company who phoned just 100 landlords (all their own clients) who had used a Section 21 notice in the past. They asked the

100 landlords why they had used a Section 21. Two per cent admitted that it was in response to a complaint about repairs, and 28 per cent said it was due to rent arrears. The other 70 per cent of the responses were unaccounted for. Perhaps – we cannot know – they used the oft-quoted 'relationship breakdown between landlord and tenant', a phrase used to conjure the idea of a marriage, subject to uncontrollable emotional forces, rather than a contract to pay money in return for the provision of a home.

In fact, the report was so biased that Alex Hilton, then director of Generation Rent, emailed the members of the APPG to express his concern. As he pointed out in his email, the report (though neither a formal committee report, nor independent) would be quoted from when the amendments were discussed in the upcoming Deregulation Bill, the bill that the measures in the failed Tenancy Reform Bill were later added to. Lib Dem MP Annette Brooke, a member of the APPG, also expressed her concern to the group's Chair, asking that the report be removed.

But Baron Richard Best, another member of the APPG and of the House of Lords, says the timing was strategic. 'It was the usual problem', he says. 'Everyone gets sent the report and given a few days to comment, and because everyone's so busy, they don't get around to seeing that email and commenting in time. So the author of the report has to – I say *has* to; I mean *is delighted to* – carry on without changing anything.'

The Residential Landlords Association

The Residential Landlords Association has 18,000 members, who each pay a membership fee of between £80 and £159 per year in return for free advice. Local authorities are encouraged to join for free. They have an annual turnover of £1.7 million, and, according to their company report, assets of around £600,000. Their 23 paid staff are divided into advice, admin, marketing and public affairs teams, and in 2015 they appointed housing lawyer David Smith as head of policy. In a press release from his law firm Anthony Gold, Smith said he 'looks forward to leading the RLA's policy work, to secure the best possible outcomes for our members'. He will remain a practising solicitor at Anthony Gold, taking on cases brought by tenants against their landlords.

Landlords who sign up to an organisation are more likely to come from the law-abiding end of the spectrum, but not always. When the RLA published its 'Top Ten Tips for Landlords' in March 2015, it hit the national headlines in all the wrong ways. Not only did the tips advise landlords to turn up at a prospective tenant's house, unannounced, to 'see how they live' (a practice that housing lawyer Giles Peaker described in the *Independent* as 'tantamount to stalking'), they also advised landlords to issue a Section 21 eviction notice on the day the tenant moves in, to save time in evicting them once their six- or twelve-month tenancy has expired (a practice outlawed in the Deregulation Act, which had passed through Parliament in the same month). Speaking to the *Independent*, Peaker said the tone of the guidelines betrayed the attitudes of many landlords towards tenants. 'Every single one of [these tips] regards the tenant as a potential menace', he added.[2]

In the north London pub, Alan Ward grimaces when I mention it. He repeats what he told the *Independent*, that it was an administrative 'cock up', adding that the staff member who published it 'has been dealt with', though they kept their job.

Still, he advocates landlords being choosy, and boasts that he interviews 30 tenants before he selects 'the right one for me'.

Ward repeats the usual lines: that private renting is already far too regulated, that the existing regulations only need to be enforced better, that tenants are the real problem. But he is an odd bundle of contradictions. He does not consider it a problem that house prices have locked a sizeable chunk of society out of homeownership, forcing them to rent privately. 'I don't see anything wrong in renting as opposed to owning', he says, but later tells me he bought his son a flat when he reached his thirties so that he wouldn't have to rent any more. A few minutes later, he denies that anyone outside London is priced out at all (in fact, recent government research shows that it's a severe problem in Oxford, Cambridge, Brighton and all other major UK cities, as well as rural areas including Cornwall, Herefordshire and Norfolk. Nationally, the average house price is now nearly nine times the average yearly income, ruling out mortgages based on salaries.[3])

When asked why so many landlords struggle to see their property as their tenant's home, he says that's not the problem; it is *tenants* who fail to see it as their home. But he dismisses as 'unworkable' the argument that the legal minimum tenancy should be increased beyond six months. He says tenants ought to form an emotional bond with their rented home, because then 'they're more likely to respect it'. When I ask if he believes emotional bonds can be formed on six-month tenancies, he replies, testily, 'Yeah, why not?'

Shelter's proposals for a five-year tenancy, which the tenant is free to leave with two months' notice while the landlord can't evict during the five years, are, he says, 'not fair', and this is not the only point in the interview where he sounds like a petulant child who wants all the sweets. He praises the four nurses who have 'nested' in one of the five shared houses he lets, but he only gives them two months' security of tenure at a time, on a rolling periodic contract.

In fact, he's almost impossible to have a sensible conversation with. Ask a straight question, and you get a startlingly tangential answer, or some wildly irrelevant statistics (many of which are produced by the one academic, Michael Ball, Professor of Urban and Property Economics in the School of Real Estate and Planning at Henley Business School, who carries out all of the RLA's research). We talk about energy efficiency for a while. He recognises that some renters are forced to pay over the odds for their fuel or – in some cases – go without heating, because their rented homes aren't insulated. The problem is, he says, there's no financial incentive for landlords to insulate their properties.

'Isn't there a moral incentive?', I ask. Instead of answering, he swerves onto carbon monoxide poisoning. 'How many people die from carbon monoxide poisoning a year? Nine! Only nine people! But landlords are having to come up with carbon monoxide sensors now!' he says, indignantly.

Despite having fought the Tenancies Reform Bill tooth and nail, he insists the RLA is happy with the slightly revised version of it that eventually became law. But minutes later, he doesn't seem sure where he stands. I ask him again whether he thinks tenants should be protected from eviction if they've complained about genuine disrepair in their home. There is a long pause. Eventually, he says 'I think tenants should be protected from illegal evictions.' I explain that illegal evictions are already illegal, and that I've asked him about retaliatory evictions, of which most types remain legal. 'No it's not', he says. 'If it's retaliatory, it's illegal.'

Bizarre as is it to have to explain the difference between retaliatory evictions and illegal evictions to the head of an organisation that campaigned against one being turned into the other, I plough on, explaining that my own former landlord, who evicted me for asking for a new chest of drawers, still has the legal right to do so despite the slight restrictions introduced by the new law. 'We need Section 21 until there is an effective way of gaining possession on grounds of anti-social behaviour, non-payment of rent, or illegal activity. The existing process [for eviction on those grounds] doesn't work', he says, and I'm relieved that at least this is starting to feel like a coherent argument. 'So, theoretically, if there were something that allowed the landlord to evict easily for those things, there would be no need for a no-fault eviction, right?' I ask.

'No, I'm not saying that.'

'What other grounds should there be, if the tenant isn't at fault?'

'Well ... [he pauses] ... the mortgage lenders might need it. The tenant might be paying the rent, but the payments might not be going to the lender.'

'You mean when the landlord isn't paying the mortgage?'

'Yes, possibly.'

'But that would be the landlord's fault, wouldn't it?'

'Yes.'

'I'm just trying to work out what moral case there could be for landlords having the legal power to evict someone when they haven't done anything wrong.'

'If everything else is legal and above board, I don't think I can argue against you on that. Your landlord should not have evicted you for asking for a new chest of drawers.'

'But he did have the legal power to do it. Do you think that he *shouldn't* have had the legal power to do it?'

'Sometimes people abuse the law. There's got to be a balance where it can be a benefit to landlords who are within their rights to seek possession.'

'And you think they should have the legal right to do it when the tenant hasn't done anything wrong?'

'Yes. Possibly. Section 21 still has a valid use.'

'Possibly?'

There is a long silence. When he doesn't reply, I offer to fill the silence. 'It's interesting, because it's unique to the UK', I say. 'Is it? I don't know', he says, unconvincingly.

It's hard to measure truly the effectiveness of any lobbying organisation. But housing campaigners who sit in meetings with civil servants and landlord lobby groups say the DCLG is growing visibly tired of the RLA's dogged tone. A look at the RLA's website suggests that if they and the government were once the best of friends, things might have become a bit one-sided lately: a blog post boasts of Ward's most recent meeting – five days before the 2015 summer budget – with housing minister Brandon Lewis, complete with a snap of the two shaking hands. 'The minister outlined the government's housing timetable', says the post, failing to mention the cuts to buy-to-let tax breaks that were announced five days later.[4]

Slick or not, when you've got the money to pay lots of staff, it's easy to make sure there's a speaking slot at conferences, to churn out reports and press releases, and to fill local newspapers. Just before the 2015 general election, an opinion piece written by the RLA, declaring that 'Tenants in [X] are being let down by a bidding war between some parties about who can clobber landlords the most. Such a tone is cheap politics that achieves nothing', appeared verbatim in several local newspapers and websites in Manchester,[5] Brighton[6] and Liverpool,[7] with the name of the relevant city pasted in.

The National Landlords Association

Not all landlord bodies briefed against the Tenancies Reform Bill. The largest one, the National Landlords Association, didn't, though publicly it came out against it. Its chief executive Richard Lambert says it wasn't that they were happy with the bill, but that they realised it would get through eventually, having been given the government's support in principle, so they made a strategic decision to 'work with' civil servants on the details later. I ask him about the two MPs, Davies and Chope. 'On that day, I watched and thought: 'that's a Pyrrhic victory'. Whoever it was that briefed those MPs to talk the bill out may be very pleased now, but they will regret this', he says.

The NLA has 27,700 members who each pay an £85 annual membership fee. There are 30 paid staff in the main office, plus a network of 38 regional representatives who are paid part-time to represent the NLA in their local area. Then there's a team of 18 paid telephone advisers, who work on a rota. The NLA runs training courses for landlords and offers services including tenant referencing, landlord's insurance and mortgages. It also runs the MyDeposits scheme (the only one of the four compulsory deposit protection schemes that allows landlords to keep their tenants' money in their own bank accounts, so that it accrues interest for the landlord), and a special insurance policy offering cover in the event of a tax inspection from HMRC.

Lambert runs me through the profile of the average NLA member. Nationally, 70 per cent of the UK's landlords own just one rented property, but the average NLA member owns between four and nine. The average member is in their fifties or sixties, receiving £53,000 of rental income per year from ten tenants, as well as a household income of £48,000 from work or sources other than rent. They spend 63 per cent of their rental income on costs (for example, mortgage interest, maintenance, furniture and insurance) and have a portfolio worth £1.2 million.

In 1997, the year of New Labour optimism, Lambert went to work as a lobbyist for the British Property Federation. A card carrying member of the Labour Party himself (and, curiously, not a landlord) his view of private renting is in many ways the embodiment of New Labour values: that housing wealth is something to be relaxed about, that the free market simply needs a socially responsible face, that profit – rather than regulation – is what will encourage people to do the right thing.

He agrees that private renting needs more stability and higher standards, but he disagrees that the burden should be shouldered by landlords. In fact, he even objects to the recent changes to tax breaks for buy-to-let landlords, having calculated that the cost to the average landlord will be £840 per year. It's wrong, he says, that buy-to-let mortgage holders should have to follow the same rules as those who take out mortgages to buy homes for themselves to live in. He admits that 15 per cent of all mortgages are now buy-to-let, and that this figure is growing rapidly, but this, in his view, is a good thing.

'The Bank of England has warned that buy-to-let poses dangers to the housing market, hasn't it?',[8] I ask. 'Frankly, I don't understand the Bank of England's concerns', he says. 'What concerns me more is that 30 to 40 per cent of the population, regardless of their housing tenure, cannot afford their housing costs from their own resources. That's a much bigger problem.' 'That's mostly because landlords are charging such high rents, isn't it?', I ask. 'Um …' he hesitates. 'They don't necessarily. Some charge under the market rate. Our surveys show most tenants haven't had a rent increase in the last twelve months.' 'Twelve months isn't very long, is it?' 'The affordability issue is across the board, not just in the private rented sector', he replies.

We go round in circles for a while, as I point out that, with interest rates at an all-time low, and private rents at an all-time high, it's not rising mortgage payments that are causing landlords to put the rent up. Each time I bring up any form of rent control – there are many sensible models that work well in other market economies in Europe – he assumes I'm saying that landlords should make a loss. In fact, most modern forms of rent control would still allow landlords to make a profit; just a smaller one.

Like the RLA, the NLA's line on regulation is that we don't need more of it, just better enforcement of existing rules. You might think that this would mean they support local councils, who have most of the responsibility for enforcement, but you'd be wrong. When Newham Council in east London became the first council to introduce mandatory landlord licensing, the NLA fought hard against it. 'We got stick from our members about being too easy on Newham, despite all the work we did: we organised consultation meetings, we lobbied, we paid a five figure legal bill to take legal advice about bringing a judicial review against the council. But we didn't stop it.'

The NLA organises local meetings for landlords in boroughs considering landlord licensing, so that they can campaign against each council individually. When Newham's neighbour, Enfield, announced their plans to adopt a similar scheme, one landlord stumped up considerable funds to bring a judicial review against the council, arguing that the public consultation was invalid as it hadn't included residents of neighbouring boroughs. 'That guy is a just a data geek – he only did it because he was angry that the council had misused data', says Lambert.

In future, the NLA plans to work on changing the image of landlords, which Lambert says is unfairly negative. On increasing the membership he says that it's hard to reach the vast majority of landlords who do not see the need for legal education or services. 'What do they read? Where do they gather?', he asks rhetorically. 'They're everywhere; they're ordinary people. The biggest challenge we have is reaching the people who don't think that they're landlords. There are lots of people who say "I'm not a landlord, I just let out a couple of flats."'

The NLA attends the meetings of the RLA-run All Party Parliamentary Group on private renting, but only follows it loosely. 'APPGs are not a route I've ever been keen to go down, as a lobbyist', Lambert says, adding that the NLA prefers to focus on civil servants rather than parliamentarians, and that if they ask for a meeting with a minister, they usually get it because it's easier to get one as a membership organisation. 'If you can build up your credibility and kudos [in the civil service], it helps get your case across.'

When the NLA publicly criticised the way the funding for the Green Deal had been handled (it was suddenly pulled six weeks after its launch), senior officials from the Department of Energy and Climate Change phoned to describe the changes they'd made based on the NLA's advice, and to thank them for their dialogue. Lambert says the NLA had 'several' discussions with Emma Reynolds, then shadow housing minister, about Labour's proposals for renting reform in the run-up to the 2015 election, but won't disclose the details, other than that he thought the proposals were 'unworkable'. Tenants simply don't need security of tenure, he says, and besides, 62 per cent of NLA members said it would 'seriously damage' their business.

'Losing the right to no-fault possession', he says, 'was actually the biggest concern among our members about Labour's proposals. Because no-fault possession is the one thing that gives them...' – 'Power?' I interrupt – 'No, no. It's the one thing that gives them confidence. *Confidence*', he repeats, adding that procedures for eviction when the tenant actually is at fault are inadequate. The problem with the amendments to the Deregulation Act that restrict no-fault eviction when there is a repair problem, he says, is that it will lead to huge numbers of invented complaints from renters, who will also deliberately

damage their homes in order to be protected from eviction for
six months.

Most NLA members see landlordism as a way to fund their
pension, Lambert says. So does he see it as a social problem
that, according to a recent report from Pricewaterhouse-
Coopers, by 2025 more than half the population under 40
will be stuck in private renting? After all, this means they'll
be paying directly for their landlord's pension with very little
chance of ever having their own. 'We've got a new generation
of people coming into the market with student debts. Are you
seriously asking them to take out a massive amount of debt for
a mortgage?', he asks, swerving the question. Will he be happy
for his children to be private renters, when they are older? 'I
don't think they're going to have any choice', he says, adding,
when asked, that he doesn't know yet whether he will help them
onto the property ladder. But is he confident they'll be treated
decently by their private landlords, without further regulation
of renting? 'Um … no, because you can't be confident about
anything like that. Nothing ever runs smoothly.'

Lambert insists that private landlords are doing society
a favour by 'providing homes'. He dismisses the idea that if
landlords were to exit the market, those same homes would
be available for first-time buyers and house prices would start
to come down: first-time buyers and landlords want to buy
different types of homes, he says. 'They may come down, but
would they come down enough?', he asks. 'And at what point
would the two thirds of the population who own property start
to say to the government "you're destroying our investments
and our children's inheritance"?' 'So housing policy is based
on the interests of property owners stacked directly against the
interests of those who can't own property', I say. 'Certainly, that

would appear to be the overriding concern of government', he replies.

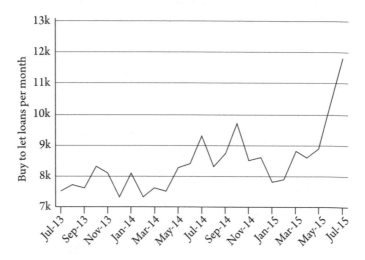

Figure 2   Buy-to-Let Lending is Soaring

Source: Council of Mortgage Lenders

'Landlords tend to be people who vote'

Labour leader Jeremy Corbyn meets me in Finsbury Park, a few days before he announces his party leadership bid. He has been a reluctant member of the RLA's All Party Parliamentary Group since it began in 2011, when he became concerned that the tenants' case was not being heard. 'I didn't really want to join it', he tells me. 'I didn't like the terms of reference of the group. It's very one sided.' But he joined so he could be part of their cross-examination of Essential Living, a property company catering for students in his Islington constituency.

'When I go to those APPG meetings I'm made to feel very unwelcome', he says.

Corbyn is a staunch defender of renting reform, having tabled several private members' bills, asked questions in the Commons, and taken time to meet his local private renters' group – Islington Private Tenants – to offer practical support and encouragement. He laments the failure of the Tenancies Reform Bill, and describes how he tried to persuade his colleagues to be there. 'We could have got the hundred MPs', he says. 'My worry is that, with the current level of buy-to-let mortgages, the growth of private renting and the lack of regulation of it, and the huge levels of profit that are going to be made in it, we're reaching a stage where there's a politically critical mass of financial interest in private renting.'

He is not referring to the other critical mass – the few parliamentary constituencies where renters outnumber property owners. He means there are too many voting landlords with too much to gain financially from an unregulated market. 'If the current trend continues, we're going to be looking at 25 to 30 per cent of the nation living in the private rented sector. Unless something dramatic happens, like big landlords moving in on it, which could take a while, you're looking at several million people letting out one or two flats. And they can become a politically significant group. Particularly in marginal constituencies. So you find all the parties trimming towards them: landlords tend to be people who vote.'

He praises the new crop of private renters' groups. 'They're on the ball, and sharp to pick things up. Emily [Thornberry, the other MP in Islington] made a speech about housing the other day in the Commons, and I intervened to ask about private renting to make sure it gets on the parliamentary record – and immediately there was stuff on Twitter showing support. It's impressive.'

But he is concerned that the message is not yet filtering through to the nation's 11 million private renters. 'Locally, my experience of the private renter vote is that they're over-whelmingly Labour voting, but there's a very low rate of voter registration – it's a very high turnover of addresses. They're quite hard to see, and not easy to get hold of. I'm more likely to come across private renters through an online petition about a different issue – and then they might write back and say "Oh by the way I'm a private tenant."'

'There was £240 million of tenants' deposits sloshing around in the back pockets of landlords'

The struggle against the landlord lobby goes back a long way, and even the most minor rights have been hard won. Before 2007, there was no obligation for a landlord or agent to protect a tenant's deposit: until then, these sums, usually equivalent to a month's rent, were considered by landlords to be a gift or a one-off non-refundable fee, as there was no legal mechanism for the tenant to claim them back.

Liz Phelps, the housing policy specialist who eventually won the battle to introduce the Tenancy Deposit Scheme, requiring all deposits to be registered and deductions to be arbitrated by an independent third party, says the process took ten years. It began in the early 1990s. A policy specialist at the National Consumer Council (a quango that later became part of Citizens Advice) was bewildered to discover, on moving to the UK from Australia, that no deposit protection scheme existed. He spoke to Phelps, then working for Citizens Advice, who thought the idea had potential and began to gather evidence. 'It was a neat policy package to try to sell, because there was an obvious solution and it was self-financing, so no government money was needed', she says.

She found parliamentary support in the Lib Dems, but it was a chance encounter on a train that swung things in her favour. Coming back from a conference, she found herself sitting next to a senior civil servant. 'It was a complete coincidence. It was a long train journey, so she was a captive audience', says Phelps. 'In the end, she said "Ok, I'll tell you what we'll do: we're just looking at changing the questions in next year's English Housing Survey [the government's annual housing survey], so I'll try and get a question in there about deposits and see how big the problem is."'

The figures came back: there was £240 million of tenants' money 'sloshing around in the back pockets of landlords', entirely unregulated. In 1997, New Labour entered government and said they'd be willing to consider a deposit scheme, but that, as they were reluctant to regulate, it had to be tried on a voluntary basis first. A pilot was set up. At this point, Phelps came up against the Association of Residential Letting Agents (ARLA). 'Their head cornered me and explained – or, at least, I soon worked out – that the way a lot of letting agencies were running their businesses was off the deposit money. He was dead against the idea of a custodial scheme, because it would completely undermine their business model.'

The voluntary scheme, unsurprisingly, rolled on for a few years without much take up. Like any voluntary regulation, oxymoronic by definition, it looked set to fail and was threatened with closure. So Richard Best – head of the Joseph Rowntree Foundation and one of the first 'People's Peers', becoming Baron Best in 2001 – stepped in. He twisted the arm of Charles Falconer, then minister for housing, persuading him to inject another £250,000 to keep the pilot scheme alive. 'It didn't cost Charlie anything and it was just getting me off his back', says Best. 'I was moaning on, making a fuss and asking questions on the floor of the house.'

But when preparations for the 2004 Housing Act began, deposit protection was not mentioned anywhere in the proposals, so Phelps began lobbying, with the help of the Lib Dems and Baron Best. 'We could prove that it worked in other countries, like Canada and Australia. But the landlord lobby was incredibly opposed to it', says Phelps. 'When I talked to them, and tried to get to the heart of what the problem was, I saw it was an emotional attachment to having this money. They more or less said that to me. It's *feeling* the money, it's saying "*it's mine*". They would actually say things like "You don't understand the importance of us having this money", and I would say "Well, I think I do actually. The point is that it's the *tenant's* money."'

At that time, Phelps says, the British Property Federation and the Association of Residential Letting Agents were at the more professional end of the landlord lobby, while the others were considered amateurs. 'They certainly wouldn't have had an APPG or anything like that back then', she says. 'They hardly knew their way into the House of Commons.' Nevertheless, she would personally receive ten-page emails from the RLA, desperately trying to rubbish her evidence. And when Baron Best established an informal private renting policy forum, where housing experts could discuss evidence and ideas, the housing experts were eventually crowded out at the meetings by representatives of the landlord lobby, who would turn up uninvited while people had to go and find more chairs for them to sit on.

Deposit protection was included in the 2004 bill and became law. Rather neatly, the scheme included some protection from no-fault eviction: if a tenant's deposit had not been protected in a recognised scheme, then any Section 21 that the landlord issued would be invalid. 'We had tried to get protection from no-fault eviction into the 1996 bill, but it was quashed. It was such a sensitive area, because it goes right to the heart of the imbalance of power. Landlords saw it as their fundamental ace', says Phelps. 'So when I saw in 2014 that Sarah Teather was going for it, I thought "good for her, but does she know what she's up against?"'

'Private landlords allow the government to turn a blind eye'

Baron Best, without whom Phelps says she could not have got the deposit protection regulation off the ground, is a key supporter of housing reform and not just in private renting: he's credited by some housing policy campaigners as the person who coined the term 'bedroom tax'. I phone him at home to ask about the landlord lobby. 'You're right that they try to influence things, but it's pretty ineffectual stuff', he assures me. 'They're pretty third rate, and everyone knows they only represent about 2 per cent of private landlords. It's not that that holds back renting reform. It's because the government knows that with things as they are, there's nowhere else for people to go. The government doesn't want to put its hand in its pocket [to provide housing]. Private landlords allow them to turn a blind eye.'

'The tide is beginning to turn'

When the deposit protection scheme finally came into force in 2007, few renters were aware of it – or of the ten-year struggle to bring it in. Back then, such things were minor issues and renting reform a niche subject. For many, the penny had yet to drop.

Speaking to me a few months after the Deregulation Act was passed, containing most of the proposals from the Tenancies Reform Bill, Martha Mackenzie, public affairs officer at Shelter, says she thinks the tide is beginning to turn. 'The biggest change I've seen in the last three years is the step change in what the DCLG is willing to do about renting', she says. 'Of course, the Conservative victory and manifesto was extremely disappointing, with its emphasis on Right To Buy and no mention of private renting reform. But now, there's a sense in government that renting is actually a problem. Even as recently as 2012, Grant Shapps [then housing minister] was saying "renting's fine, everyone loves the flexibility and freedom". And it's been amazing, seeing so many renters talking to government, chipping away at those perceptions.'

She thinks the shift in attitude coincided with the DCLG's 2013 select committee inquiry into private renting, which, though typically understated, finally acknowledged issues that campaigners had been talking about for decades – such as revenge eviction. 'The issues got a really good airing, and it led to the government's own review of poor conditions in the private rented sector. Everything that's happening now, I see as a direct lineage from that point. There was Bob Blackman, an extremely right-wing Conservative MP [and member of the CLG select committee], coming out in favour of the Tenancies

Reform Bill. He actually went and talked to some of those case studies in person.'

However, she says, the landlord lobby still enjoys a level of access to government that is hard to comprehend. Partly, this is because they're overwhelmingly white, male, middle-aged landlords talking to other white, male, middle-aged landlords, with all the thigh-slapping and rapport that that entails. But, she thinks, their grip is loosening. 'They're not as smart as they think they are, and self-preservation is their number one goal at all times – which doesn't make them very good influencers. The RLA, for example, just puts out an endless stream of press releases that are absolute nonsense, and I think people in government are starting to cotton on to it.'

Even under a Conservative government, Mackenzie thinks there will be some progress on renting reform, albeit minor. New Zealand, currently a favourite among Tories due to its right-wing prime minister who increases his majority at every election, is starting to crack down on the buy-to-let market, introducing minimum standards and making it harder to get a buy-to-let mortgage than a homeowner one. 'When they see that a right-wing government is willing to intervene on that level, Tories here think "Ooh, we could do that too"', she says.

The other key shift, Mackenzie says, is that renters themselves are becoming more vocal. When in March 2014 Shelter asked people to send in their stories of revenge eviction, they received 250 fully written stories within the first 24 hours.

'We need people having rational conversations in policy circles, but we also need people shouting on the street'

Another shift that occurred in 2014 was the launch of Generation Rent, a national campaign group specifically for private renters, set up with a £600,000 grant from the Nationwide Foundation. Tasked with making private renting the primary issue in the 2015 general election, it based much of its strategy on identifying the constituencies where renters outnumber homeowners, trying to use them to swing the vote in favour of Labour, with its proposals to offer three-year security of tenure, rent increases linked to inflation, and a ban on letting agent fees.

But Generation Rent faced huge challenges. Occupying an uncertain ground between the policy-making process and street-level protest, it was unclear whether Generation Rent should aim for insider or outsider status. With funding to pay for just five full-time staff, it lacked the infrastructure to support any local campaign groups – and whether voluntary activists are truly the route to policy change is a moot point. Its first director, Alex Hilton, drew admiration and criticism in equal amounts when he pulled out of the Homes For Britain campaign, a campaign staged by the larger housing associations and the landlord lobby, which pledged, vaguely, to 'End the housing crisis within a generation' and floated a giant inflatable house carrying the slogan over London.

But the bigger challenge is uniting the nation's 11 million private renters, who span all age groups, incomes, educational and professional backgrounds, and all types of political outlook and culture. Traditional trade union style organising models can't work when each renter has a different landlord; there's no mechanism for collective bargaining in the way that there is in a workplace, or in a social housing block owned by one organisation. With 70 per cent of the UK's private landlords letting just one home each, private renters are scattered as a political group.

Betsy Dillner took over from Hilton as director in 2015, when the Nationwide Foundation pulled its funding – a shock that forced the organisation to become a media campaign run by just two staff. Dillner came to the UK from America in 2012 to study community organising. Having worked on a campaign to save a charity housing project (the closest the US comes to social housing in the European sense), she was surprised to discover how 'antagonistic' the UK housing debate was. 'That campaign was in New York City in 2007, at the height of the housing boom in the US. People were making money left right and centre, in the way that they are in London now. But in terms of political structure, we had a Congressman who was helpful and a Democrat-run city council. And city councils aren't under the same pressure as local councils are here', she says.

Because the community in question (housed by a charitable housing trust that wanted to sell up) was already 'tight', and already had the same landlord, the campaign to save it was winnable. Dillner and her colleagues prevented the sale four times, then secured a change in legislation to protect its affordability for the next 40 years. But changing private renting in the UK has proved to be harder. This is partly due to the landlord lobby, she says, but not necessarily because of their strength or skill. 'It's always a lot easier to gain power with people you already agree with. Successive governments always say we just need to let a free market sort everything out, and lots of private landlords to let out homes because otherwise who will provide them, and that just falls straight into the landlord lobby's hands. So they don't really need to do too much to get power.'

Despite this, she thinks the conversation has changed, and has found some landlord organisations easier to work with than others. 'It's been easier to engage with the NLA than the

RLA, for example, because at least the NLA is willing to admit that some things should be changed.' And there is always some common ground to be found, even between opposing groups: the new 'Right to Rent' legislation, which forces landlords to become quasi border guards and take responsibility for the immigration status of their tenants, is disliked by landlords and renters alike – though their reasons reveal their true attitudes.

Dillner says she 'spoke to the RLA saying "look, this is something we could potentially work together on", and Alan Ward said "Well, all *we're* concerned about is what happens to the landlord when their tenant gets deported and the landlord isn't allowed to rent out their property any more."' For Dillner, a migrant herself, this stings. 'I really worry that the housing market is going to become so unsustainable that central government will discharge local government of all legal responsibilities to house homeless people. It sounds crazy, but I come from America and that's what *we* do. So it's not impossible for people in power to justify it to themselves. That's the thing I really love about Britain and the reason I want to stay here, because there is still a sense that we rise and fall together, that you don't let people die in the streets on their own.' There is a crack in her voice. 'And I see that culture being chipped away.'

Differences over strategy have impeded the renters' movement: while there is a growing number of local groups for private renters, each has different focus and style. Some prefer the educational route, teaching renters about housing law or offering emotional support to people being bullied by their landlords. Others act as informal enforcers, rooting out bad landlords and telling councils and local media about them. Some actively engage in the policy-making process, while others refuse to do so, insisting that street-based protest must be the only tool used and that those in power must not be spoken to.

'It's natural for there to be disagreement internally among movements', says Dillner: 'We need people having rational conversations in policy circles, but we also need people shouting on the street. Those things have to happen in tandem. One of my biggest peeves is the mis-telling of the story of the civil rights movement in America, as if it was just a beautiful thing that sprang up with no conflicts, and leaders who had no flaws. That's not actually what happened. There was a huge rift between Malcolm X and the non-violent contingent, but Malcolm X got people scared, and that gave Martin Luther King more power.'

With the general election behind it, Generation Rent is reforming to have an elected, rather than appointed, board of trustees, and if it can find sustainable funding it will focus on closing the gap between policy makers and those affected by their policies. 'My guess is that the MPs and civil servants who are landlords themselves are probably decent enough landlords, so they just can't see the problem,' says Dillner. They find it easy to believe that landlords never abuse the law, because they never do it themselves. But the whole point is that you don't make policy based on the people who are doing everything right. You base it on the people who are doing everything wrong.'

Turning victims into activists

While local housing protests have always attracted seasoned activists, many of the UK's 11 million private renters are finding themselves spurred into action for the first time.

Richard Duxbury is from a Conservative-voting family and had never been on a protest before he moved to London to work in the film industry. He and his partner found themselves living in a flat with mice, rats, cockroaches and flies coming from the derelict building next door: the letting agent who had shown it to them had taken advantage of their limited time, showing them the flat at night and promising that it would be completely renovated before they moved in. Once they had signed up, all renovation plans vanished and the agents stopped returning their calls.

When their local trade union branch handed his partner Sophie a flyer for a housing debate, the couple didn't feel it was aimed at them, but they were so frustrated by the conditions in their flat that they went along to hear the speakers. There they met other private renters in their borough, Waltham Forest, who were already part of an informal network of other local renters' groups. A few weeks later, Duxbury found himself in a meeting with Labour's shadow housing minister Emma Reynolds, discussing the party's proposals for renting reform.

The Waltham Forest group now meets their local council to press them to enforce the council's new landlord licensing scheme, and works with the local Green and Labour parties and trade union groups to organise public debates. Duxbury is a regular spokesman and has helped set up a similar group in the neighbouring borough of Redbridge. 'The audience I'm speaking to is me, eighteen months ago', he says. 'I was just a renter who was unhappy, having terrible experiences of renting, but with no history of activism. I wanted to do something about it but didn't really know what to do. Now, I just see a huge constituency there who can be turned from passive victims of the housing crisis into activists.'

A borough-based renters' group can put pressure on its local council to do more to tackle bad landlords, and focus on the nitty-gritty details that might go unnoticed by broader campaigning. When the Consumer Rights Act came into force in May 2015, requiring letting agents to display all their fees up front or face a £5,000 fine from the council, few agents expected anyone to care. But Waltham Forest Renters surveyed all the letting agents in their area, finding that 21 of the borough's 56 agents were breaking the law, and handed the details to the council.[9] They also designed an online fee checker so renters looking for flats in the area could compare local agents' fees, which ranged from £150 to £792 per tenancy.

But with minimum contracts of six or twelve months, renters often have to move between boroughs. Richard and Sophie's letting agents did not renew their tenancy after the couple complained about the conditions in their flat, and installed new tenants instead of carrying out repairs, so the couple found a flat in another area.

Jacky Peacock, a veteran housing campaigner who has run a renters' group in Brent since the mid 1980s – gaining an OBE for services to private renters in 2001 – says her job was easier when renters had security of tenure and rent control, as it meant they were a settled part of the community and organisers could focus on specific neighbourhoods. But even then, expectations were still low. 'In one flat I lived in, our landlady would come round hammering and screaming at our door to collect the rent', she says. 'The door was flimsy and once, it came off in the landlady's hand. Somehow, we didn't think that was outrageous.'

Peacock's group got some funding from the Greater London Council, and then from Brent Council after the GLC was abolished. But funding remains the biggest challenge for local renters' groups. Local campaigning is time-intensive, and most people these days have to squeeze it in around paid jobs. Some of the younger groups draw lines between themselves and funded projects, refusing to work with anyone who is paid – which, in turn, blocks the building of a unified voice. The Brent renters' group, now known as Advice4Renters, acts as a solicitor agency with its own fee-charging solicitors, but recent changes to legal aid have forced them to look elsewhere for funding. 'It's just an endless battle to bring the money in', Peacock says.

Brent Council has introduced landlord licensing in three areas of the borough. Advice4Renters, with some new funding from anti-poverty charity Trust For London, has been going door to door to speak to renters about the scheme, but most have not heard of licensing nor the extra protections they have as a result. The council itself has invested in staff to implement and enforce the scheme, but for the 30,000 licensed homes there are 25 council staff to carry out inspections and enforcement. This means licenses have been granted to substandard homes: Peacock describes one that she visited as 'little more than a corridor', with a kitchen in the middle making it impossible to escape in the event of a fire – and no smoke alarm. Now that it has the power to do so, Peacock thinks the council should take on the management of the worst privately rented homes themselves.

London councils have responded differently to the emergence of new renters' groups, depending on the focus and style of each group. While the Brent and Camden renters' groups, established in the 1980s, get funding from their councils in return for providing renters with housing advice, other groups choose not to engage with councils at all, while others want a critical but constructive relationship. In Hackney, the local renters' group, Digs, used the council elections in May 2014 to begin their relationship by collecting the testimonies of 50 private renters in the borough, presenting them to councillors and using the 'dossier' to start conversations at a local election hustings. Then, when local elections were over and the new council in place, the group sent mock eviction notices to all the newly elected councillors, telling them they were being evicted from their jobs, to highlight the lack of security for renters.

Renter activism is not limited to London. In 2014, Generation Rent set up local groups in Brighton, Manchester and Liverpool, funding part-time organisers to raise awareness and secure media coverage of renters' experiences. In Edinburgh, the independent Edinburgh Private Tenants Action Group used the 2014 Scottish Housing Bill to engage renters by asking them to sign the group's consultation response, and ran street stalls collecting 2,000 signatures. They formed the 'Living Rent Campaign' – a broad alliance of trade unions, faith groups and community groups – calling for the implementation in Scotland of the Dutch system of rent control, where an independent panel rules what rent can be charged based on a home's features and quality, and on local amenities. The Living Rent campaign is also working on a Tenants' Manifesto for the 2016 Scottish Parliament elections.

In Northern Ireland, campaigns for fair renting have started in student unions. Adam McGibben began campaigning when he was a student in Belfast after a string of bad experiences. 'One house was just black mould', he says, 'and there were holes in the single glazing'. Progressive legislation on housing in Northern Ireland has lagged behind the rest of the UK, he says, due to the Troubles: deposit protection, for example, was only introduced in 2012. 'Where we could, we tried to get good existing legislation brought over', he says. One legacy of the Troubles, he explains, is that private landlords are even less accountable than they are in Britain: land registry data, which allows renters to identify the owners of specific houses, is not made available to the public for security reasons.

When McGibben was elected to his student union, he set up a union-run letting agency so that students could avoid paying high fees to commercial agencies. If agencies raised their standards, they could, in return, use the brand of the student union to reassure their customers. But because the university was reluctant to put up the capital for the agency, McGibben's project was forced to partner with an existing letting agent, who used the brand without raising standards. Students complained, and eventually the agency was shut down. 'If it's going to work, it needs to be an entirely student union-owned operation', McGibben says, adding that student unions in Birmingham and Sheffield have managed it. In hindsight, he says, he should have organised more protests against specific landlords. 'But how do you get that collective power and collective bargaining when you are dealing with hundreds of one-man bands?'

While the tide may be turning, it remains a long way out. Young movements, whether they emerge from student unions or elsewhere, face the same impediments: members are still learning social skills, and finding out about politics and power. Some are more concerned with excluding those unlike themselves than with building a persuasive argument. When it comes to renting, this is counterproductive: private renting traps people with salaries of £50,000 a year, impoverished migrants crammed ten to a room, and a hundred categories in between. They need to be united, but some can see only their differences. In the confusion, some attack symptoms rather than causes, the message becomes muddied, and councils who do the most to protect private renters are demonised for the shrinking of council housing – usually a result of national rather than local policy.

Activism is never perfect; neither is professional campaigning. But housing groups – whether they seek to change policy or simply to protest – are raising awareness of inequality among a generation for whom renters' rights have never truly existed. It usually takes a no-fault eviction or a sudden rent increase to make an otherwise apolitical renter understand the position they're in, but these days – unlike a decade ago – that renter may well find a local renters' group to turn to for advice and support, even if only on social media. And while landlords still have the money to fund their political lobby, they can't win the argument forever.

CHAPTER SIX

The History of
Private Renting

Samir Jeraj

Most private renters would not deliberately risk being taken to court by their landlord. But when 49 people in Glasgow were served with a court summons for non-payment of rent, representatives of the local trade unions met with the judge in advance of the hearing. They warned that if they were convicted, there would be a strike across the city. After a brief hesitation, the judge dropped the charges.[1] This was 1915, and those 49 people were part of a 20,000-strong rent strike that changed housing in the UK.

At the start of the twentieth century, one in five people owned their home. The rest paid rent to a landlord: usually a private individual, or, for some, a philanthropist providing a Victorian version of social housing. Like today's 11 million private renters, the renters of 1900 lived drastically different lives from each other. At one end of the market, elegant townhouses in Bloomsbury catered for the Bohemian set; at the other sat rows upon rows of slum terraces, destined to be demolished by councils over the coming decades.

The two-way relationship between poverty and housing had just begun to interest social researchers, and it was York that set the scene for Seebohm Rowntree's investigation

Poverty, A Study of Town Life. As New Labour would do 100 years later, Rowntree set a 'decent homes standard' and used it to asses the housing he found before him. His verdict? Nine in ten people in York were living in housing conditions that fell below 'decent'. He wrote: 'It has been shown that 4705 persons are living more than two to a room, whilst the actual number of those overcrowded, whether viewed from the stand-point of health or of decency and comfort, must be much larger than this. We have seen that the rents, although much lower than in many other towns, swallow up an unduly large proportion of the income of the poorer sections of the working classes, the proportion thus absorbed being no less than 29 per cent in the case of those families earning less than 18s. weekly. And finally, we have seen that York, although a comparatively small city, contains slums which are probably as bad as any to be found in London.'

On average, private renters now spend 47 per cent of their 'take home' pay on rent – in London this rises to 72 per cent, according to the English Housing Survey 2013–14[2] – more than Victorian renters were. Friedrich Engels, in *The Condition of the Working Class in England*, documented the poor conditions and high rents in 1840s London slums: 'The abominable dwellings in Drury Lane, just mentioned, bring in the following rents: two cellar dwellings, 3s., one room, ground-floor, 4s.; second-storey, 4s. 6d.; third-floor, 4s.; garret-room, 3s. weekly, so that the starving occupants of Charles Street alone, pay the house-owners a yearly tribute of £2,000, and the 5,566 families above mentioned in Westminster, a yearly rent of £40,000.'

In Manchester, too, Engels railed against the 'slum landlords' who rented out unsanitary housing: 'The landlords are not ashamed to let dwellings like the six or seven cellars on the quay directly below Scotland Bridge, the floors of which stand at least two feet below the low-water level of the Irk that flows not six feet away from them; or like the upper floor of the corner-house on the opposite shore directly above the bridge, where the ground-floor, utterly uninhabitable, stands deprived of all fittings for doors and windows, a case by no means rare in this region, when this open ground-floor is used as a privy by the whole neighbourhood for want of other facilities!'

Long before Clement Attlee set about building a million post-war council houses, Victorian social reformers were busy setting up charities and 'friendly societies' to house the poor. These provided relatively small amounts of housing compared to today's equivalent organisations, housing associations, but they were early examples of social housing later taken up and developed on a large scale by councils. When American philanthropist George Peabody built the first Peabody Estate in Spitalfields in the 1860s to 'alleviate the condition of the poor and needy', the trustees told the *Birmingham Post* on its opening that decent housing would 'foster superior social habits'. Weekly rents for the 66 flats ranged from half a crown to five shillings a week – the equivalent of £5.40 to £10.79 in 2005.[3]

In November 1864 *The Daily News* noted that several of the shop units on the ground floor were still empty, but pronounced the estate 'an experiment which has been eminently satisfactory'. Under the stewardship of a former soldier, whose job was to collect rents and enforce rules, the tenants included a charwoman, a bookbinder, a nurse, a policeman, a basketmaker, a warehouseman and a mechanic. The unnamed journalist wrote glowingly of the apartments:

'We found ourselves in a comfortable, well furnished little apartment, wherein every article, from the highly polished mahogany drawers and near sofa, to the small shelf of books and the framed certificate of odd fellowship or forestry on the walls, spoke of well-to-do prudence and prosperous thrift.'

A year after its opening, the trustees declared in the minutes of their meeting that aside from a single eviction due to an 'unruly husband', there had been a 'manifest improvement in the habits and manners of both old and young'.[4] Slum clearances, spurred on by cholera epidemics in the 1860s, got under way. The 1875 Artisans' and Labourers' Dwellings Act enabled councils to clear and redevelop slums, but it also required them to rehouse their inhabitants, providing local authorities with loans to pay for it. By 1904, 80 towns had borrowed £4.5 million for clearance and redevelopment, but 2 to 3 million people still lived in slum housing in 1914.[5]

The Boundary Estate in Shoreditch was one of the first council housing developments. Built by London County Council in 1900, it was on the site of 'The Nichol', a once desirable suburb but a slum by 1880. London's population was growing, and a lack of housing regulation meant houses were overcrowded, poorly maintained by landlords, and badly served for sanitation. Increasingly difficult for politicians to ignore, housing had gained the attention of parliament, and by 1885 the Housing for the Working Classes Act was passed, giving the Local Government Board the power to shut down unhealthy housing and making it illegal for landlords to rent out homes that failed to meet a basic standard of sanitation.[6] Two years later came the Boundary Street Scheme Act, enabling the demolition of The Nichol and its replacement by the Boundary.

In keeping with the Victorian model of philanthropy, which saw social welfare not as a right but as a gift from benefactors who could dictate their terms, Victorian-style social housing came with strings attached for the tenants. No pubs were included in any new developments, and the existing twelve pubs were demolished.[7] New housing was not just to improve physical conditions: it was to raise standards of behaviour, and was provided for the better-off working classes, such as skilled artisans, clerks and small business-owners.[8] The lower orders, who could not behave, stayed in privately rented slums.

Tenant revolution

The 1900s and 1910s were turbulent decades, and many of those involved in political struggles as part of the Labour Movement were renters. In Glasgow in 1915, the political mobilisation of the working class, combined with rising rents, led to a rent strike. At the outbreak of the First World War, workers flowed into the city to work in factories. In response, landlords raised rents beyond the means to pay. The working-class tenants decided not to take it, and vowed to pay rent only at the original rate. Beginning in Govan, a district in the south-west of the city, the strike soon spread across Glasgow.

Women played a leading role in organising the strike, and the campaign drew in Labour, socialist and communist political activists. The Glasgow Women's Housing Association had formed a year earlier in 1914, and the Labour movement had been campaigning for municipal housing since 1885. One of the women who founded the association, Mary Barbour, who had first come to Clydeside in 1896, led the Tenant Defence

Association, encouraging tenants to put notices in their windows declaring that they would not pay increased rent.[9]

Evictions began, and were met with violent confrontations. In Spring 1915, the McHugh family were under threat of eviction, owing £1. At the time, three family members were serving in the armed forces and one had been wounded. When the landlord's agents arrived to serve an eviction notice on Mrs McHugh and her five remaining children, a crowd gathered to help them. The protesters nailed a Union Jack across the door, and then burnt an effigy outside the offices of the agents. The Police advised the civil court authorities to halt the warrant for fear of a riot.[10]

By November 1915, around 20,000 tenants were on strike.[11] Forty-nine rent strikers were served with a court summons to appear on 17 November, and political unrest threatened to spread into the factories and dockyards. Protesters came to the hearing, and trade union representatives met the judge beforehand and persuaded him to drop the charges.[12]

Most workers in Clydeside worked in munitions factories, and, as the First World War took hold, both factory owners and government feared disruption to production. Evictions of munitions workers, and of the families of soldiers, ramped up the hostility towards landlords.[13] By the autumn of 1915, protest had spread to Aberdeen and Dundee in Scotland, Belfast in Ireland, and Birmingham, Birkenhead, Northampton and London.[14]

Back in Glasgow, there was a continued threat of industrial action. The government feared a strike in factories, following industrial disputes in the Glasgow shipyards and munitions factories since the start of the war. Chancellor Lloyd George had written to the solicitors pursuing the 17 November rent strikers to ask them to drop or delay until new legislation could be passed.[15] Days later, on 25 November 1915, Parliament passed the Rent Restriction Act, which fixed rents at pre-war levels for the duration of the war and for six months after its end. Rent control was to last, in one form or another, until 1989.

Homes for Heroes

Though council housing would truly come into its own only after the Second World War, it began after the First. In the 1920s, partly out of continued concern for the 'deserving poor' (and to prevent the working classes looking to newly established Soviet Russia for answers), the post-war government announced they would build 'Homes for Heroes', passing the 1919 Housing Act (known as the Addison Act) to allow councils to build their own housing.

In East London, London County Council bought 300 acres of land in Dagenham, Barking and Ilford and began work on the Beacontree estate in 1921. It took ten years to build 27,000 homes for more than 100,000 people.[16] At the time, it was Europe's largest social housing estate. Most of the incoming residents came from Limehouse, where a slum-clearance programme had demolished their homes. But over the following decades the drawbacks to the development became clear, and a lack of health, education and social facilities took many years to address. Similar estates built on the outskirts of towns were often far away from jobs and services, causing isolation for many of those who were resettled there following slum clearance.

Budget cuts meant less than half of the 500,000 originally promised Homes for Heroes were actually built, but further

Acts in 1924 and 1930 granted councils money to build, and obliged them to clear remaining 'slum' housing.[17] By the outbreak of the Second World War, 1.1 million homes had been built, and one in ten people lived in council housing. These homes were largely modelled on the 'Garden City' ideas of Ebenezer Howard: detached cottage-style houses with large gardens and green space. The Department of Health laid down national guidelines specifying that homes could not be built more than twelve to an acre in urban areas, and eight in rural areas.[18] Barry Parker, who designed the Wythenshawe estate in Manchester, said his vision was 'to secure around the house the air space requisite for health, to grow vegetables and fruit for our table ... to surround ourselves with pleasant places in which to live and work, rest and play, and to entertain friends'.[19]

The council housing revolution: 1945–79

During the Second World War, bombing destroyed an estimated 218,000 homes and damaged a further quarter of a million beyond repair. There was an estimated shortage of 2.1 million homes by 1945. Housing was in short supply, and demand was growing. The government seriously considered nationalising all rented housing, such was the scale of the housing crisis.[20] In July 1945, a group of 400 war veterans who became known as the 'Brighton Vigilantes' took the law into their own hands, and began moving families into empty housing on military bases. Within weeks the government had passed a law allowing local councils to requisition empty 'residences', and the Vigilantes dissipated.[21]

In the north of England, too, people began moving into abandoned military housing. The movement spread, encouraged by coverage in newsreels. By August 1946, tens of thousands of people – mainly ex-servicemen and their families – had moved into abandoned military bases. The squatters were supported by the Communist Party and Labour Party members and activists. By September, squatters had begun to use not just military bases but empty flats and hotels. The 8th September 1946 became known as the 'Great Sunday Squat', when nearly 1,500 people occupied flats in London. The occupation of private property provoked central government into action, and five organisers were arrested and charged with 'conspiring to incite and direct trespass'. But the judge was sympathetic, and instead of issuing a penalty, gave them a 'binding over' – a behaviour order similar to the anti-social behaviour orders (ASBOs) of the late 1990s. He said: 'I am satisfied the motive was primarily to find homes for these unfortunate people.' In October 1946, almost 40,000 people were living in squatted homes.[22]

The Labour government eventually decided against nationalising the rented housing stock, but began a massive programme of council house building. These developments learned from the mistakes of inter-war housing, and included shops, public transport and services. Anuerin Bevan, then Secretary of State for Health and Housing, placed restrictions on the development of private housing.

Over the next 35 years, the supply of council housing expanded until it made up nearly a third of all housing, lifting millions out of poverty. Councils were generously subsidised to build high-rise estates, and by 1979 the UK had 4,500 tower blocks. But from a peak in 1979, the decline began. In the rush to build high and quick, standards had slipped. The Macmillan governments of the 1950s reduced the size of homes and encouraged cheaper construction methods with the aim of building more. Macmillan compared his housing policy, known as the Great Housing Crusade, to seeing 'runs stacking up on the chalkboard' at a game of cricket.[23] In Birmingham, Housing Minister Anthony Crosland approved a scheme to build 4,000 homes in one and half square miles on a former air base, and, according to the leader of Birmingham City Council, gave him a 'tongue lashing' for asking that one of the former hangers be kept as a community centre.[24] But it was not just space standards that were sacrificed. In May 1968 there was an explosion at Ronan Point, an east London tower block built using new methods and finished just months earlier. The building collapsed on one side, injuring seventeen people. Had the explosion been on the other side of the building, the human cost would have been worse; as it happened, the affected side was where the living rooms were, and most people were asleep in their bedrooms when the explosion happened.

On other high-rise estates, crime and social problems added to the poor quality of the housing, and some began to call tower blocks 'slums in the sky'.[25] The decline of industry and the edge-of-town locations of the more neglected estates contributed to unemployment and exclusion, which combined in the 1980s with policies designed deliberately to concentrate vulnerable tenants in outlying estates. Some specific areas were targeted for investment and succeeded in reviving communities, but the stigma that linked council estates with crime lasted well into the twenty-first century.

Investigations began to expose corruption and collusion between councils and the building industry. In 1974, a court sentenced Newcastle Council leader T. Dan Smith to six years in prison for accepting bribes from developers.[26] Later, it emerged that this practice was widespread – a discovery that led to the resignation of Reginald Maudling, then Conservative Home Secretary, who had business links with John Poulson, the architect who also served a prison sentence for his involvement.

The ownership revolution

The sell-off of council housing is most commonly attributed to Margaret Thatcher, but in fact it first began in 1970 under the Heath government.[27] It started with a trickle: around 7,000 households bought their council homes in 1970, rising to 46,000 by 1972. The 1970 Conservative manifesto set out their vision for council home sales: 'We will encourage local authorities to sell council houses to those of their tenants who wish to buy them. Thus many council house tenants of today will become the owners of their own homes tomorrow.'

By 1974, the Conservatives were fighting the October election on a promise of 'a new deal to every council tenant'. Tenants who had been in their home for three years or more would get the right to buy their homes at a price one third below market value. Nor were these ideas confined to the political right. In 1977, Labour Housing Minister Peter Shore published a draft policy setting out how the government should support homeownership, describing it as a 'strong and natural desire' that 'should be met'. Shore's plan was to create shared equity schemes similar to today's shared-ownership model, and to expand the role of housing associations. But he believed councils would remain the main provider of social housing.[28]

Sale levels were low in the 1970s, but rocketed in the 1980s after Thatcher was elected. This had not always been Tory policy: Conservative governments of the 1950s had competed with Labour over how much council housing they could build. The Macmillan government in the late '50s and early '60s focused on quantity over quality, setting targets of 300,000 homes to be built a year. For Macmillan, council house building was a pathway to ownership for the working classes, as well as a route out of the slums. But Thatcher's new vision of the UK as a 'property-owning democracy' was far more radical (though it was Conservative Scottish MP Noel Skelton who had coined the term in the 1920s, believing that the masses should be inoculated against socialism and communism by giving them a financial stake in the status quo).

The UK's housing stock saw privatisation on a massive scale. The 'Right to Buy', established in the 1980 Housing Act, allowed any council tenant who had lived in their home for five years to buy the freehold or leasehold at a substantial discount. Crucially, it restricted councils' ability to replace sold stock by building new housing. This was a huge blow to local authorities, who saw their rental income decline and were only allowed to invest a quarter of the sale price back into housing.[29] Instead, the duty to build social housing was transferred to housing associations.

In 2013, 33 years after the 'Right to Buy' was enshrined in law, an investigation by the *Mirror* newspaper found almost four in ten of those former council homes sold under right to buy were being rented out for profit by private landlords.[30] Right to Buy had transferred the ownership of a large chunk of the nation's housing from public to private, but the new owners of former council homes had not become owner-occupiers. They had become private landlords.

During the 1990s, TV channels were saturated with programmes about buying housing and renovating it to increase its value. Homes became properties, and the supposedly British obsession turned from having a home to owning one of ever increasing value. By 1997, Labour were broadly committed to the policies introduced by previous Conservative governments: expanding homeownership, encouraging councils to outsource the management of housing stock, and supporting housing associations as the main providers of new social housing. Labour poured billions into schemes to modernise existing social housing stock, but on the condition that councils transferred housing management to Arm's Length Management Organisations (ALMOs) or housing associations. Council house building remained very low through 13 years of Labour government, a total of 7,870 homes.[31]

Private renters and rent control

Rent controls introduced after the First World War were not intended to be permanent, or part of a plan to give renters any rights other than a fixed rent. Allowing moderate rent increases, controls remained on the statute books but did not apply to newly built homes. The controls were popular with landlords, whose interest payments were fixed. In fact, when the Conservative government of the 1920s phased out rent controls there was opposition from both landlords and tenants. Rent controls returned in 1939, and lasted until 1954.[32]

In the 1950s, the Conservative government weakened rent controls. The 1954 House Repairs and Rent Act exempted new homes from rent control and allowed small rent increases for existing homes if they were deemed to be in good condition.

The following 1957 Rent Act removed controls for valuable properties and empty homes. This encouraged landlords to evict their existing tenants and hike up the rents for new ones. But unlike today, no-fault eviction was not allowed. Instead, to empty their properties of tenants, landlords used intimidation, force and violence. One particularly unpleasant landlord, Peter Rachman, became the most infamous for using these techniques.

Rachman, a Polish refugee, spent much of the 1950s building a property 'empire' in London. Changes to rent control laws, the banning of street prostitution, and the proliferation of unregulated building societies (the letting agents of their day) created an environment in which Rachman could rent single flats and bedsits to sex workers to finance his purchase of rent-controlled housing. Many of Rachman's new tenants were recent immigrants from the Caribbean. It was legal to discriminate openly on racial grounds until 1968, and many of these new immigrants found councils and private landlords alike refused to rent homes to them. Slum landlords' techniques, which forced out white tenants to replace them with black ones, stoked racism and civil unrest.[33]

In 1964, the incoming Labour government swiftly reversed the 'decontrol' policies of the Tories, and protected tenants from harassment and eviction. The 1966 Labour manifesto boasted of its progress so far: 'In addition to restoring security of tenure to every decontrolled house, we are appointing rent officers and rent assessment committees for fixing fair rents. The new Act also gives basic protection to almost everyone in his home, including the lodger and the worker in his tied cottage. Today it is a crime not merely to evict without a court order but to harass or to persecute anyone in order to force him out or force his rent up.'[34]

The 1977 Protection from Eviction Act set out the legal definition of landlord harassment as 'acts likely to interfere with the peace and comfort of those living in the property, or persistent withdrawal of services that are reasonably required for the occupation of the premises'.[35] The Act still applies today.

Another 1977 Act, the Rent Act, created 'protected tenancies' with regulated rents, secure tenure, and succession rights – meaning private renters could pass on their private tenancy to a relative after their death. Private renters could ask the rent officer at their local council to set a 'fair rent' for their privately rented home. This would be the rent charged unless the landlord carried out major renovations, or if the landlord appealed after a period of two years. Fair rent was determined by an assessment of the local rental market but, crucially, adjusted to take into account how many privately rented homes were available in a particular area. In the 1980s, as homeownership boomed and social renting had not yet depleted to its existing levels, the private rental market shrank – which meant that the 'adjustment for supply' produced lower rents.

But in 1988 everything changed. Private renters in tenancies that began before 1989 are still protected today, but these now account for only 100,000 households in the UK. A trickle of these still appeal to rent assessment committees when they face rent increases, and the committees base their decision on the condition of the home – not necessarily on the renter's ability to pay.[36]

The boom in homeownership and the wide availability of social housing through the 1970s and '80s meant that levels of privately rented housing stock continued to fall. Opponents of rent reforms today argue that any form of new regulation will have the same effect, conveniently overlooking the more obvious causes for low levels of privately rented housing during that period. There was less privately rented housing then because there was less need for it: the expansion of council housing, building societies and other state-supported home-ownership policies meant that people who had been private tenants simply had better housing options available to them. Between 1914 and the 1980s, a quarter of privately rented housing was demolished in slum clearances, and half was sold to owner-occupiers.[37] Besides, experiments in partially removing rent controls in the 1920s, '30s and '50s did nothing to boost supply.

The 1988 Housing Act abolished more than 70 years of rent regulation in the hope that the free market would provide quality, quantity and affordability for a more mobile working population. Creating the now standard six-month Assured Shorthold Tenancy (AST), it allowed rents to be set by the market and for landlords to evict a tenant without reason, and with just two months' notice.

Debating the bill in Parliament, Conservative minister Norman Lamont said the new assured shorthold tenancy would: 'allow a tenant and landlord to agree any rent that they choose. We believe that that is right, because the best way to arrive at a reasonable rent is to allow it to be determined by competition and market forces. In the past we have seen, all too clearly, attempts to restrict rents causing properties to leave the private sector or not to appear in it, so that people who wanted to rent and were willing to pay a market rent found that no property was available. Indeed, there has been almost no worthwhile investment in private rented property for 50 years, and the sector is declining considerably.'

But a Liberal Democrat MP, Alan Beith, responded: 'I believe that by the means that they have chosen the government will open the door to the worst sort of private landlord. Instead, they should use a carefully tailored device to attract private capital back into rented housing, but ensure that that is done in a way that will provide adequate security and rent protection to tenants.'[38]

The Rent Trap developed quietly and slowly. For the first decade or so after the 1988 watershed, the effects were slight. But as Britain failed to build houses, pressure began to build. As social housing became more scarce, more people moved into privately rented housing. The costs of housing benefit – the state payment a renter of any type can claim if they can't cover the cost of their rent – spiralled between 1990 and 2010 as public money paid rent to private landlords. Conservative and Labour governments introduced policies to expand homeownership and free up access to credit, encouraging people to take out mortgages they might later find themselves unable to pay.

Introduced in 1996, the 'buy-to-let' mortgage allowed borrowers to borrow sums based not on their own earnings, but on the rental income they could charge. A new class of landlords emerged, buying up housing stock intended for owner-occupation and turning it into highly lucrative privately rented bedsits or rooms in shared houses. There is no duty for these landlords to be on any register, but tax receipts estimate that there are now more than 2 million of them in the UK.[39] The next chapter explores the effects of their actions on social relations.

CHAPTER SEVEN

The Inequality Machine

Rosie Walker

'Is a landlord with integrity a contradiction in terms?'
Tessa Jowell, 2 July 2015, Labour London Mayoral hustings

In February 2012, a landlord called Patrick Osborne told the *Guardian* that his conscience had got the better of him: he was giving up being a landlord.[1] 'It's not nice to profit from someone else's need to sleep somewhere', he told the newspaper, explaining that the imbalance of housing wealth all around him in London, and the realisation that so many people are now trapped in private renting, had made him feel uncomfortable. 'I think it's wrong some landlords have strings of properties. It restricts supply, and tenants have very few rights, or aren't aware of rights they do have ... It's wrong. I don't want to be part of that, even in my small way', he said.

Osborne was a 'good' landlord. He gave his tenants six months' notice rather than the required two, charged less rent than he could have charged, and took standards seriously. But it was the wealth transfer that niggled. He did not lose out financially when he gave it up: he sold his rental property (on which his tenants had been paying the mortgage) for £230,000, having bought it for £95,000 in 1999. He used the profit, which he admitted was 'handsome, even after capital gains tax', to pay off most of the mortgage on his current home. 'The only reason I could buy when I did, and become a landlord, was down to luck and timing', he adds. 'I couldn't afford the house I'm living in if I had to start now.'

Most classifications would describe Osborne as an 'accidental' landlord because he originally bought the house to live in himself, moving to another one later. But, crucially, when buying his second home he knew it would be more profitable to let the first home than to sell it – and he is too honest to accept the 'accidental' label. 'I'm not going to pretend I fell into it by accident. I made an active decision to do it for income and pension planning', he told the *Guardian*.

When I interviewed an anonymous landlord for a research project in 2012, one line of his stood out among everything else. Assuming he was giving me advice on how to set myself up as a landlord, he boasted about his 6 per cent yield and said he insists on certain brands of white goods in order to get a 'B Plus class of tenant, and never drop below a C Minus'. Then he added: 'I don't want to be *friends* with them. It's not that kind of relationship.'

In recognising the relationship as a business one rather than a social one, he lacked the urge to control every aspect of his tenants' lives – unlike the users of Landlord Referencing or TenantID, companies that encourage landlords to disclose details of their tenants' 'lifestyles' (including, if they choose, sexuality, relationship status, religion or friends) to other landlords. The legality of these sites is protected by a clause slipped into the small print of some tenancy agreements, and, crucially, the method: landlords only post a tenant's identifying details. Then, if another landlord recognises them, they are put in touch with the first landlord, and the two have a private telephone conversation.[2]

But there was something interesting about the way the landlord with the white-goods tip didn't want to get too close to those he was profiting from, as if looking them in the eye might have snagged his conscience. I began to wonder about the relationship between landlord and tenant, and how others see it. When one is effectively buying an asset for the other, does it help to be friends? Or is it better to keep a distance?

'It's just the market'

With no requirement to be on any register, it's hard to get a true picture of the nation's private landlords. Those who are easy to find – through landlord membership organisations, for example – represent less than 2 per cent of all landlords. The government's private landlords survey, which ran four times between 2001 and 2010, sampled a thousand landlords whose contact details were provided by their tenant, if their tenant had been surveyed as part of the annual English Housing Survey. Shelter also surveys landlords regularly.

What about the others? What about those who don't think of themselves as landlords? We talk about 'good' and 'bad' landlords with little clarity about what these terms mean. A good landlord, presumably, obeys the law, keeps a home in good condition, pays tax on their rental income and speaks politely to their tenants; a bad or 'rogue' landlord doesn't. But when it comes to economic inequality, social relationships and wealth transfer, things are less clear. A 'good' landlord, who would never dream of a no-fault eviction, who would drop everything to fix their tenant's broken boiler, might easily charge a rent that leaves their tenant little to live on, let alone anything to save. But that, they might tell themselves, is not their problem. That, they might think, is 'just' the market.

The 'housing crisis', most would agree, is a bad thing: a generalised social problem with multiple and complex causes, like poverty or conflict. But few are willing, or able, to see their part in it. Blame the lack of house building, we say, or the financial crash of 2008. Blame the banks, the green belt, immigration, family breakdown. Don't, whatever you do, blame ordinary people who simply choose to turn the situation to their advantage. And don't, under any circumstances, consider the social consequences of that advantage.

I wanted to probe the way these relationships work, and the psychology behind them. So I spoke to some 'good' landlords, some of whom let rooms or flats to their friends. All the landlords in this chapter agreed to speak on condition of anonymity, so all names have been changed.

Every landlord interviewed here vocalises a concern for social problems, treats other people with respect, and most vote Labour or Green. None would ever dream of the kind of acts committed by landlords at the criminal end of the spectrum. But when it comes to asking about money, how much of it changes hands and under what circumstances, most are reticent. When the figures are coaxed out of them, most see the rent they charge as something separate from the way they behave as a landlord, as if that part is not an act of volition. Several struggle to use the word 'landlord', preferring 'owner', or, in cases where they live in the same home as their tenants, 'flatmate'. If things have ever gone wrong between themselves and a tenant, they always 'asked them to leave' rather than 'evicted' them.

Most call what they're doing 'an informal arrangement', perhaps unaware that when rent changes hands, laws apply regardless of what's written on paper. And the 'informality' does not appear to work both ways; rent must be paid, and on time. Some display a surprising level of self-deception: a live-in landlady with a mortgage of £390 per month insists she pays a third of it herself, while charging her tenants £550. And when asked why they do it, 'it makes sense' is a common answer.

It's as if, when it comes to property, we've disconnected our actions from their social consequences. We prefer to see market-driven inequality as random, chaotic, like a game of snakes and ladders. As if the housing game is so absurd that the moves we make within it have no meaning. But they do.

'You kind of forgive yourself if you're nice to them'

For some, becoming a landlord is a short-term solution to a practical problem. Gail, a freelance writer, and her husband Paul, a primary school teacher, spent a decade renting privately in London, at one point having to move home three times in a year. When, in their early thirties, Gail became pregnant with their first child, Paul's parents stepped in, providing a deposit which, when combined with an inheritance Gail had been left from a family friend, came to £80,000. In 2012 they bought a small ex-council flat in east London for £230,000, paying a monthly mortgage of £650 – a far lower amount than they had ever paid in monthly rent.

After two years, Paul got a new job in Bournemouth. Cautious about trying out a new city, they decided to rent a home at first, and let their east London home. 'We looked at the rents going on Gumtree and pitched it as high as we could', says Gail. They chose not to use a letting agent, advertising it online and downloading a template tenancy agreement after a Google search. They let the flat to four tenants, the same age as themselves, who pay a combined rent of £2,000 per month, with council tax and fuel bills on top. The £1,350 difference between their mortgage payment and the rent they receive is almost enough to cover their rent in Bournemouth, too. 'The discrepancy will be really useful when I'm on maternity leave', says Gail, who is expecting her second child.

Asked how much her tenants are paying as a proportion of their income, Gail says she doesn't know. 'But we were slightly alarmed when we found out that one of them only earns £9 an hour in a chicken shop. It's terrible isn't it? I've become one of those horrible landlords! But you kind of forgive yourself because we're nice to them and we're honest.'

Gail and Paul do not plan to be landlords for long; they intend to settle in Bournemouth, buy a home there and sell the east London flat to pay for it. They say they would repair anything that needed it, and would only evict their tenants if they became nuisance neighbours. But their experience shows how easy it is to charge high rent to people who would otherwise be your peers, with little knowledge of your legal responsibilities. I ask if they have protected their tenants' deposits – which come to £2,000 – in a recognised protection scheme. 'No', Gail says, sounding guilty. 'But we had to pay a £4,000 deposit on the house we're renting down here, so to have £6,000 of our money tied up would be ludicrous. We're not going to *not* pay our tenants back, though. I only recently found out that we're actually breaking the law by not protecting it.'

I don't point out that £2,000 of this £6,000 is actually their tenants' money. Instead, I ask how she feels when she reflects on the housing situation in the UK. 'I definitely feel worse after this conversation! I'm part of the problem', she says. 'I am, really. If you don't want to be part of the problem, you have to set the rent below market rates because market rates are ridiculous and everyone knows that. But maybe in ten or twenty years' time we can be nice good social people, when we've got a bit of money in the bank.'

'I do find it quite conflicting. But I'd probably add on a few hundred a month next time'

With 'market rates' (meaning the maximum amount that someone who needs housing will pay if they have to, rather than any indicator of quality or choice) at sky high levels, it's easy for someone charging 'below market rate' – perhaps, say, £50 less than the landlord down the road – to feel that they a have social conscience.

Simon, a research administrator in his thirties, bought a £215,000 flat in east London in 2007 when he inherited £35,000 from his grandmother. After he and his partner had lived in it for four years, they took a year off work to go travelling and let the flat through a letting agent, using the rental income to fund their travels. When they returned, they continued to let it – swapping the tenants for friends who wanted to rent it. The letting agent was 'a little bit pushy, but quite positive' about the area's new status, and this might have contributed to their decision to remortgage the flat on a buy-to-let mortgage, with another £30,000 from Simon's father. Crucially, it was an interest-only mortgage – which meant that, as buy-to-let landlords, they could make the entire monthly mortgage payment tax deductible. Using that flat as capital, they bought another flat in south London and moved into it themselves, paying £800 per month on the mortgage there.

They charge their friends in east London £1,200 per month, excluding bills, of which £700 goes on the buy-to-let mortgage, leaving £500 to cover the lion's share of the mortgage on the home they live in, too – though Simon assures me that some is spent on maintenance costs. According to Zoopla, the original flat is now worth £477,000, but Simon says he wouldn't sell.

Asked how he sees his part in the bigger housing picture, Simon squirms. 'I do feel very lucky. I don't earn very much, and I feel it's awful for people who work as hard as me, or who earn more than me, who will never be able to get on the property ladder. I find it quite conflicting as well.' He prefers renting to friends because they make improvements to the property themselves and it 'feels more positive'. 'I'd be happy to rent to strangers again, but if I did, I would probably add a couple of hundred pounds on, per month', he says.

Like Gail and Paul, Simon has only ever needed a loose grasp of the legal rights and responsibilities of tenants and landlords. He explains that he left all that to the letting agent when he went travelling, and now that he lets to friends there's no need for a 'formal contract', seemingly unaware that proof of rent paid – for example, though a bank statement – acts as a contract, giving any tenant a de facto Assured Shorthold Tenancy (AST) with all the standard conditions. When I ask under what circumstances he would evict a tenant, I have to explain that unlike in most other countries, no-fault evictions are legal in the UK in most cases. 'I didn't know that. So landlords have the right to evict you?' he asks.

'We pay high rent where we live, so we're being f***ed over as well'

Some who let to their friends prefer arrangements where they live in the same house. Kim was working in an admin job in Brighton in 2003, earning £22,000 a year, when her parents encouraged her to buy a house, giving her a £95,000 deposit for a two-bedroom house at £190,000. Because she planned to live in it herself, she used a residential mortgage rather than a buy-to-let – but moving tenants in was always the plan. 'I definitely needed the income from the tenants to cover the mortgage – I wouldn't have been able to cover it all myself', Kim says.

So why did she choose to do this, rather than buy a home with a mortgage that she *could* afford to pay herself? 'That was just the decision', she says. Kim turned the living room into a third bedroom and moved two friends in. Aged 22, she'd had little experience of being a renter herself, as she'd lived with her parents while at university. Though some live-in landlords choose not to pay a share of their own mortgage, Kim stresses that she paid a third of the 'rent' herself because it 'didn't seem right' not to. But a few weeks after our interview, when I press her for figures, it transpires that she charged her two tenants a total of £550 between them per month, while the monthly mortgage payment was £390. The amount she paid was just a sum going into her own bank account. It was, I think, something she needed to tell herself to ease her conscience.

She says it was sometimes difficult to maintain friendships with the people who were paying her mortgage, and, although she always accepted that maintenance was her responsibility, felt annoyed when others didn't do the cleaning. 'It's definitely an odd situation to be in', she says. She's still a landlady, and she's had only four problems in 12 years: one tenant disappeared while another three were asked to leave with a month's notice because they were no longer able to pay their rent. One of them had nowhere to go, so Kim let him stay on a little while longer until he found somewhere.

After ten years, Kim moved to London, where she now rents a two-bedroom flat with her partner and a friend, for £1,900 per month (excluding bills) between them. 'So we're being f**ked over as well', she says. Her parents paid off the remaining mortgage on the Brighton house, and Kim now charges £1,220 a month in rent, split between her three tenants, and thinks that being a landlady is easier at a distance. She has, reluctantly at times, dipped into the money she gets from the rental income, and says she would have struggled without it, earning £23,000 a year as a freelance TV props buyer.

Asked how much rent her tenants pay as a proportion of their income, Kim says she doesn't know; she doesn't ask how much they're earning before they move in. 'I assume that if they're willing to pay the rent then they can afford it', she says. Previously, in the days when her tenants were also her friends, she says it would have been 'too awkward' to ask how much they earned, though it was not awkward to collect a specific amount in rent.

'I think tenants should have more protection', she says. 'I definitely wouldn't sell up if the laws were changed to give my tenants more rights.' She adds: 'The balance is totally tipped in favour of those who can afford to be landlords. I can't see how it's going to change unless some crazy laws come in, but who wants that to happen when people are making sh*t loads of money?'

'Others are doing it too'

When I speak to Alice, she has just had a pay rise to £27,000 a year, but at 34 is struggling to pay off student loans and an overdraft from periods on a lower income. After a recent demoralising search for rental accommodation in London, where prospective flatmates interviewed and declined her, she was pleased to find a friend of a friend who owned a flat with a spare room. She pays him £720 per month, including bills.

Alice has not thought to question this amount, saying she's just glad the rent is not much more than in her last place, and she'd prefer to think of her landlord's mortgage as 'his business'. I contact him to find out. Dave earns £40,000 a year, and bought his flat 18 months ago for £420,000 with a 50 per cent deposit after he inherited some money, which brought the monthly mortgage payments down to £700 – which Alice is paying all of. 'I've only had two … er … flatmates, as it were', Dave says, adding that I must anonymise this interview because he hasn't told his mortgage provider about the arrangement. He uses the words 'casual', 'informal' and 'loose' many times to describe what he is doing. I don't ask him how he justifies the amount. Instead, I ask him how he sees this arrangement in the context of the bigger housing picture. He replies awkwardly. 'It's … er … a curious situation that you find yourself in. I've got friends who are, you know, very 'right on' and they've bought an ex-council flat to live in and now they're looking to buy another place to let out. You think, well, here are these people who tell themselves they're very left-wing, they benefited from the quintessential Thatcherite policy and now they're doing very well out of reducing the housing stock. I joke around with them about the moral implications, but it's funny. Well, it's funny if you're in that position where you can laugh at it, but I guess less so for other people.'

Later, I ask Alice why people in her situation aren't more angry, when they struggle to pay off the mortgages of others who could easily afford to pay it themselves. 'I think people recalibrate their level of satisfaction according to what they feel is possible', she says.

'It makes sense'

For some, letting to their peers is a way to change their lifestyle. When Sam was 26, he worked full-time in a record shop earning £25,000 a year. He inherited £65,000 from a grandparent and, with another £15,000 from his parents, bought a £259,000 flat in 2004, with a monthly mortgage payment of £700.

The flat, in London, has one big bedroom and a box room. Sam says it was 'never really the plan' to rent out the box room, but 'as soon as I moved in I thought "Well, it would make sense."' A university friend was looking for a home, and agreed to pay £500 a month for the box room. Sam carried on working at first, but after a few years decided to quit his job to play in bands – a move that coincided with his monthly mortgage payment dropping to £450 after the initial fixed term ended. His tenants have changed over the years, but Sam has always chosen from 'friends, or friends of friends', and always kept the rent at £500. With no housing costs to cover personally – though he's keen to emphasise that he pays for milk and fuel bills, plus £41 a month in ground rent – he can afford to get by with minimal earnings from working as a musician. He has no plans to return to work.

'I approach it in a really fair way', he says, as if fairness were a fact rather than a contested term, 'in that I can't really afford to cover all the costs. You have to strike a balance between what the market rates are, what I can afford to cover myself, and ... what they can afford, I suppose.'

Many who rent rooms from their property-owning peers are happy with the arrangement. They focus on the fact that their rent is slightly lower than it would be through a high street letting agent, rather than on the fact that they're paying most – or, in some cases, all – of their friend's mortgage for them, buying them an asset for their later life that they may never own themselves. The friend who first rented Sam's box room was eventually able to save enough money to scrape together a deposit to buy his own home, with a partner. But not everyone was so lucky.

Mates' rates

When Sam's third tenant Howard, also a university friend, hit financial difficulty, he went to work abroad on a construction project for two months. Sam planned to put a short-term tenant in Howard's room while he was away, but when that fell through, it was assumed that Howard would pay in full, despite not using the room. When the employer failed to pay Howard, Sam granted him a two-week deduction on the two-month period. Howard fell into debt to cover Sam's mortgage payments, which put a strain on the friendship.

'This is the crux of the problem when mixing friends and renting', says Howard. 'Total professionalism is expected of the renter, but there's NO expectation when it's turned around the other way. If you ask for anything, then you're "not being a friend"'. Sam eventually asked Howard to move out. 'It worked out the best for him, because his new place is less financially accommodating, so he has to take more responsibility for himself', says Sam, who has recently moved in his fifth tenant, and discovered that his flat is now worth three times its original price.

But Sam says he is concerned about the effect the housing market is having on society. 'That's my biggest worry: I've been in London my whole life and I can see the social fabric is beginning to change because of the housing situation. People are being forced out; it's a kind of social cleansing.'

Howard, who was then earning £50 a day as a cycle courier, turned to other friends, a couple with a child who had bought a £252,000 flat and had a spare room, for which they charge him the 'mates' rates' of £550 a month. 'They made me feel welcome, and living with a family was lovely', says Howard. But after a year, the couple realised they could live off the rental income if they moved to Ibiza, so they moved two more tenants in – the three paying £1,650 a month in total, excluding bills – and left for the Spanish island, where they do not need paid work.

They took care to find tenants that would suit Howard as flatmates, as they could choose from several applicants. But as soon as they left, the dynamic changed. Once, Howard mistakenly made an online transfer of £500 instead of £550 for the rent. 'That same day, I got an email from them in Ibiza saying "Hi, £50 short!" If I were in their position, I'd be cooking my tenant eggs in the morning and asking when they want their windows cleaning next, because that tenant would be paying my mortgage for me.'

When Howard broke his arm in a road accident he couldn't work for a while. He told his friends in Ibiza that the rent would be one week late while he tried to scrape together the funds, and one of them said the other might 'lose it' with anger when she found out. When I speak to Howard, he is £1,300 in debt and hasn't had a holiday in three years. His friends have given him no contract, meaning he can be asked to leave with two months' notice. He long ago gave up trying to save any money, trying instead to stay out of debt. He apologises for 'sounding bitter'.

'I think a lot of people have to try really hard to convince themselves that there isn't any iniquity to the whole situation. Whether it's a trick of the mind, I don't know. My friends make a big fuss about the ground rent they have to pay, and the wear and tear, but those are just the costs of owning a property and our rent more than covers it.'

I try for several months to interview Howard's friends in Ibiza, and although one initially agrees to it, he subsequently avoids all calls and emails.

Buy-to-let: a middle-class taboo?

It's tempting to see wealth inequality as an accident; it feels less uneasy if we do. In the world in which people born before 1975 grew up, the relationship between landlord and renter could be (though wasn't always) a benign transaction: the simple and temporary provision of shelter for an inconspicuous, proportionate rent. But in parts of the country where housing is in short supply, renter-landlord relationships have come not just to reflect inequalities, but *produce* them.

We might prefer to think that two identical 30 year olds, living in the same neighbourhood, with exactly the same job, income, education and skills, have similar economic lives. If A has been helped onto the housing ladder by family wealth and B hasn't, we'd prefer to see it as inconsequential; sometimes it's sunny, and sometimes it rains. It shouldn't matter. But if B has no choice but to hand over most of his earnings to A, to buy A an asset and a pension that B will never have, things begin to feel rather feudal.

A renter effectively pays not once but three times: first in rent, second as an unpaid caretaker of an inflating asset and third, with the freedoms they forfeit. With the silent passing of every standing order, their roles, their status – *their class* – becomes ever more entrenched, and the possibility of escape reduced. Sometimes, wealth inequality has to be carefully revealed by social scientists, using t-tests and regression analysis to unpick complex variables. But in the private rented sector it's there in sharp, zero-sum relief. And no one can bear to look.

Angus Hanton, economist and co-founder of the Intergenerational Foundation, agrees that it's a middle-class taboo. 'It's a bit like a dirty secret', he says. Hanton is a baby boomer with teenage children. Acutely aware of the role of housing in driving wealth inequality – in a personal as well as a professional sense – he says that boasting about wealth has always been considered vulgar, particularly in Britain. But the structural shifts in housing over the last few decades have produced a particular kind of inequality, and it's stark. So it's hardly surprising that those who benefit from it remain quiet.

The appearance of the buy-to-let mortgage in 1996 was no accident. Banks had been keen to lend to the growing number of owner-occupiers in the 1980s, knowing that people would keep up repayments for fear of losing their home. But the financial crash of the early 1990s, when mortgage holders lost their jobs and house prices plummeted, saw banks repossessing family homes – an experience Hanton describes as 'searing' for the banks. Turfing distressed families out onto the street looks bad. Buy-to-let mortgages offered a more attractive approach. 'From the banks' point of view, it meant that you could get the landlord to do the dirty work for you', he says. Tenants could be removed easily by the landlord, with minimal fuss, and replaced with higher-paying ones. In the worst case scenario, the property could be sold quickly. After all, it would not be the mortgage holder who was losing their home.

Banks quickly realised that buy-to-let was a much safer bet. When banks calculate the risk of lending to someone buying a home, Hanton explains, they look at primary and secondary sources of repayment and consider what borrowers could do in the event of an emergency. A homeowner only has one source of income: their job. But a buy-to-let mortgage holder has at least two sources: their job, and their tenant's job. If they have more than one rented property, they have several sources of reserve income, from several tenants – so one income stream can be moved to cover a shortfall from another, if necessary. Because buy-to-let is such a safe bet for banks, they can lend much larger amounts than they would for owner-occupier mortgages, and at lower interest rates.

The period of reckless lending from the banks between 2000 and 2007 is well documented. But many accounts assume that the reckless lending was to people desperate to own a home, overstretching themselves and egged on by the banks. In fact, a large proportion knew the overstretching would not be done by themselves but by their tenants, who would have little choice but to pay whatever rent was demanded. 'There was a tendency to turn a blind eye to this', says Hanton. 'It was a conspiracy, really, between the lenders and the borrowers, to get the business done.'

Unlike in the 1990s, after the 2008 crash the property market recovered quickly. Any losses felt by the owners were easily compensated for by simply putting the rent up – and the few owners who really were financially squeezed were able to sell into a buoyant market while their own home remained untouched.

It did not end there. To avoid inflation, the Bank of England began to slash interest rates. By March 2009, the base rate was at 0.5 per cent, a historical low, where it has stayed for the last seven years. 'That's what really put the fire under the buy-to-let market', says Hanton. Savings in the bank could earn hardly any interest; other types of investment could earn 2 to 4 per cent. But a buy-to-let property could fetch a 9 or even 10 per cent return – and that's before factoring in the capital gains from the property increasing in value, which, in many parts of the UK, was already happening again.

The fire spread, and estate agents soon realised that buy-to-let buyers were better customers. A first-time buyer, buying a home to live in, provides an agent with a one-off transaction. A buy-to-let buyer can not only pay more, but they also provide an estate agent (many of whom double up as letting agents) with further custom when it comes to letting the property, as well as the possibility of future purchases. The Estate Agents Act of 1979 laid down unenforceable regulation – such as the rule that when an offer is made on a house, the agent can't pass that information on to other buyers. This,

Hanton says, is easily got around by introducing 'sealed' bids. 'You see this happening all around the country', Hanton says. 'They set a closing date, and tell buyers to send their best and final offers by Friday, and some of those offers are leaky. So the agent can tell the buy-to-let buyer "I think if you offer X, you'll just get it." And the buy-to-let investor can nip in at just £500 above the offer from the first-time buyer.'

Agents can also steer favoured buy-to-let buyers away from bad purchases while encouraging first-time buyers to go for them, Hanton says. This goes against industry regulation, but there's no practical way of enforcing such rules. 'They have an inclination to treat first-time buyers as mugs, whereas the buy-to-let buyer is someone they regularly do business with', says Hanton. 'I don't think the technical side of things should be underestimated. But politicians do underestimate it.'

It took until 2015 for the Bank of England to warn that buy-to-let posed a threat to the nation's financial stability. By then, buy-to-let accounted for 15 per cent of the entire mortgage stock in the UK, having risen from just 1 per cent in 2000. The Bank of England's Financial Stability Report, published in July, warned that 'looser lending standards in the buy-to-let sector could contribute to general house price increases and a broader increase in household indebtedness',[3] adding that buy-to-let buyers are more likely to have interest-only mortgages, making them 'potentially more vulnerable' to interest rate rises. What it failed to mention was that the indebtedness and vulnerability would not be borne by the owners, but by the people paying their mortgages for them: the renters. And if house prices continue to rise, the two thirds of the nation who own property are unlikely to complain –

least of all the landlords. After all, rising house prices means more people for whom renting is the only option.

Just a week after the Bank of England's warning about buy-to-let, chancellor George Osborne announced modest curbs on the tax allowances enjoyed by buy-to-let landlords. But if they acted as a dampener on the flames, the effect was likely to be cancelled out by a pre-election giveaway he had announced in April that year. People in their fifties, who until then had only been allowed to withdraw a quarter of their pension as a lump sum, were now allowed to withdraw the whole amount and spend it on whatever they fancied – or whatever they felt was the best investment. As the *Guardian's* business leader warned, 'none of this is good news for first-time buyers, firmly priced out of London and soon to be priced out of a starter home – possibly by a granny'.[4] Many people choose to become landlords to supplement an inadequate pension – and we have allowed them to shrug at the fact that their tenants, in paying into their landlords' private pension pot, will do so at the cost of ever having a pension of their own.

Perhaps unsurprisingly for the co-founder of a think-tank studying intergenerational justice, Hanton sees rising wealth inequality as something demarcated along generational, rather than purely economic, lines. Despite the rise in people letting to their peers, the average landlord is middle aged while the average renter is in their twenties or thirties. But private renting is no longer only for the young: a recent analysis, by accountancy firm PwC, of the government's annual English Housing Survey predicted that if current patterns continue, by 2025 more than half of people under 40 will rent their homes.[5]

What we prefer to ignore is the role that family wealth plays. No accurate records exist on how many first-time buyers are helped by family wealth, but the Council of Mortgage Lenders make annual estimates based on the difference between buyers' salaries and the price of the house they have bought. Where there is a disparity, it is reasonable to assume that buyers have been given money from relatives, whether living or dead. In 2011, CML estimated that two thirds of all first-time buyers had been helped into ownership by family wealth. This figure had dropped to 52 per cent by 2014, though the figures are slightly distorted by the 50,000 first-time buyers who have used the government's Help To Buy scheme. Crucially, the figures do not record how those buyers plan to arrange the repayment of their mortgages: this could be done either by themselves or by their tenants. There is no need to declare any landlord status if you've lived in a property yourself at any point, and even if you haven't, checks go unmade.

Do landlords pay tax?

In September 2013, a court gave landlord Kevin Power a year's suspended sentence for tax evasion. He had rented out a north London home for nine years without paying income tax on the rent, and, when he finally sold the home, had failed to declare capital gains tax.[6]

Power was unlucky: HMRC figures suggest it is relatively easy for landlords to avoid paying tax on their rental income, despite HMRC campaigns encouraging landlords to turn themselves in in return for lower fines. A look into the figures shows how little is known about the sector that houses 11 million people – not even how many landlords there are. HMRC figures reported in the *Guardian* state that 2.1 million people declared income from property in the 2012–13 financial year,[7] but the tax office estimated in 2014 that a million landlords are still failing to do so fully – costing the nation £550 million each year.[8] In 2014 the *Telegraph* reported that only 500,000 people are 'registered as owning a second home', and that HMRC had only just begun – for the first time – to contact letting agents to ask for details of the landlords on their books.[9] The powers to fine letting agents who, when asked, do not provide information to HMRC, were only granted in 2011.

With no requirement for landlords to be on any register, HMRC must look elsewhere to find them. A spokesman for HMRC says online adverts for rented homes are a good place to start, as well as discussion forums on landlord websites. Deposits, which must be registered with a recognised protection scheme, provide a database of landlords using them – but many landlords and tenants are still unaware of the deposit protection scheme almost nine years after it became law. A discussion thread on Landlord Zone in 2013 entitled 'Deposit companies grassing landlords up to HMRC'[10] advises landlords not to take deposits at all if they do not want to be found in this way, and to simply charge higher rent instead. Mortgage providers can also be asked to provide details of people who have taken out buy-to-let mortgages, though not all landlords use them.

Tax investigators also use software to detect mismatches between a person's declared income and their property purchases, says the HMRC spokesman. This is a more useful strategy, he says, than trying to find those whose entire lives are lived below HMRC's radar. Completing a tax return inaccurately is more common than declaring no income at all.

'It's a sophisticated, nuanced approach', he says, explaining that HMRC has to make choices about who to prosecute and usually goes after the 'bigger fish'. But if 70 per cent of landlords in the UK let just one property, that's an awful lot of small fish. The Let Property Campaign, launched by HMRC in 2013, was a public awareness campaign to coax the 'small but anxious' into the net, he says, allowing the Revenue to target their resources at the bigger offenders.

When a landlord is caught, it's more cost effective to come to a civil settlement than to bring a criminal prosecution, he says, and the amount the landlord must pay is discretionary depending on how much they have evaded and how sophisticated their level of evasion was. Since civil proceedings usually take place in private, details are not made public, and HMRC will not reveal how much tax has been recouped since it began its Let Property Campaign.

Although significantly reduced by George Osborne in 2015, tax breaks for private landlords remain generous. Overall, the maximum amount of tax relief a landlord can claim on rental income dropped from 45 per cent to 20 per cent. But mortgage interest, letting agent fees, repairs and maintenance, mortgage brokers' fees, accountants' fees, ground rents, service charges and insurance all remain tax deductible, though the amount that can be claimed against mortgage interest has been reduced – and repairs and maintenance costs must now, for the first time, be backed up with receipts to prove the money has actually been spent. The rate of capital gains tax (applied to anyone who owns a second home and sells it) was not changed, and can still be partly avoided if the landlord says they have lived in the home at some point, no matter how long ago or for how long. The only new restriction on capital gains tax is that it must be paid sooner after selling.

In November 2015 Osborne announced a 3 per cent rise in stamp duty on any home bought as a buy-to-let or second home, prompting a group of 250 individual landlords to launch a legal challenge against the Treasury arguing that it breached human rights legislation. The 250 landlords started a crowd-funding campaign to raise the initial £15,000 in legal fees.[11]

As one of their membership benefits, paid-up members of the National Landlords Association get insurance against the costs of an unexpected tax investigation. The insurance won't cover the costs of any penalties if a landlord is found to have been creative with their tax return, and the NLA says that fewer than 20 of their members use the insurance each year.

Are we running out of time?

The problems of private renting are not necessarily caused by a moral failure on the part of landlords, whether they see themselves as 'accidental' or deliberate landlords. The 'common sense' that rules renter-landlord relations is a result of the availability of buy-to-let mortgages, a relaxed approach to taxing landlords and the threadbare legal rights granted to renters. These policies tell landlords that a house is an investment like any other, that the market sets the price and that your responsibilities as a landlord are really a matter of personal preference. Above all, they convey the message that being a landlord is an honest investment in bricks and mortar, rather than a way to 'trap and tap' a person who has no choice but to be trapped and tapped.

Politicians are terrified to tackle this web of contradictory 'common sense'. Policies to 'solve' the housing crisis have to operate within it, regardless of the consequences. But time is running out: in 2015 the English Housing Survey showed that more people own their home outright than ever before. This is partly due to an ageing population, and many outright owners are not landlords. But housing wealth is being spread ever more unevenly. As the gulf grows between the housing haves and have nots, so does the gulf between what passes as common sense and basic moral positions: moral positions like not profiting from friends, not exploiting the disadvantaged and not living on unearned wealth. It is this gathering discomfort and unease, felt by landlords like Patrick Osborne, that carries the possibility of change. But while a growing number of people are doing so well out of it, it will take a very brave politician to bring that change about.

CHAPTER EIGHT

What Else is There?

Samir Jeraj

Until policy makers can make life fairer for the nation's 11 million private renters – a number growing all the time – some find themselves forced to look for alternative escape routes. Some find them and discover that this is how they wanted to live all along, like young and healthy people who can live on decent boats. Most find ways to 'make do', sacrificing legal rights and decent conditions in return for slightly lower rents through property guardian schemes. Others look for longer term, collective solutions – such as community land trusts and co-operatives – that call for considerable funding and take years of hard work to establish. But these alternatives can only ever cater for a tiny fraction of the millions stuck in the rent trap.

Property guardianship

Marko (not his real name), who escaped the rent trap six months before I meet him, now shares a former leisure centre in Hackney, east London, with seven others. There's a foyer and reception area that have been turned into a kitchen and communal space, and the rules set by the company managing the building are pinned to the wall. Marko's own room looks as if it used to be an office. He admits it's small, and the management company can ask him to leave with a month's notice rather than the two he would get as a private renter on a standard tenancy. But crucially, his rent here is £400 per month – a saving of around £300 per month compared to the average price of a room in the area.

Property guardian schemes originated in the Netherlands as a way to prevent squatting.[1] Property owners (companies, individuals, or even councils and social landlords) employ a company to manage their empty property and to find people to live there temporarily. The owner has their property protected against squatting and vandalism, the company gets paid, and the property guardians get somewhere to live which is slightly cheaper and often bigger than they might get in a privately rented home. The catch? The property guardians have to sign away their rights. In law, they are licensees rather than tenants – meaning they have little right to notice when it's time to leave. And they forgo the tenant's right to 'exclusive possession', so the company or landlord can enter where they're living at any time. Sitex Orbis, a property guardian company, estimated in 2014 that 4,000 people in the UK now live like this.[2]

Lorna was a property guardian in Coventry in 2013. She found out about it through a friend who was living in a monastery, and moved herself into one of the rooms, paying around half what she had been paying as a private renter in a shared house. The building was owned by the council, had 20 rooms, six tenants and a huge garden, and cost just under £200 per month, including bills. 'It was almost unreal, how cheap it was, and it was an amazing place', she says.

But after a trust bought the building from the local council a year later, things became more difficult. The council was quick to carry out repairs and maintenance, Lorna says, but under the new ownership it was unclear who was responsible for them – the trust itself or the property guardian company. Lorna and her fellow guardians lived with a water leak that came through two floors, destroying all of one tenant's possessions. 'They just didn't do anything about it', Lorna says.

Ironically for an arrangement based on the principle that live-in guardians are meant to protect the property, security was a major concern, and Lorna experienced several break-ins. On top of that, the trust decided to open parts of the building to visitors, which meant strangers were regularly wandering through the building and doors were not being locked. Lorna describes the situation as 'unusual'. 'There was no chance to settle in somewhere, or even unpack properly, if you might be moving out in a few weeks', she says, adding that finding, buying or moving furniture was also difficult.

Lorna found it to be a good short-term solution. After 18 months, she complained about the disrepair and was evicted with two weeks' notice, but the guardian company found new accommodation for her in a former care home in Coventry within three weeks. Again, people tried to break in through windows that did not close properly, and Lorna felt ill-equipped to deal with it. 'We were meant to be the ones protecting it, but we are not security guards. We are just normal people', she says.

Gloria Dawson, an academic researching property guardianship at Leeds University, says these schemes work well as a temporary measure for some people. The spaces available – often warehouses, or disused offices – are attractive to artists looking for a cheap space to work and 'leverage their career'. Others are would-be private renters who don't have enough money for a rental deposit or the first month's rent, and use property guardianship as a way to save up for a rented room or flat. But, she says, property guardians rely on 'back up' housing, like the sofas of friends and family, to fill the gaps between properties, and she has never met one who didn't have this safety net. Many property guardians are not aware that they would be eligible for state benefits to live, or don't feel that they have the right to claim them.

Guardianship schemes market themselves in different ways. Some, such as Camelot and Live-in Guardians, focus on security, emphasising the guardian's role as a security guard, while others, such as Dot Dot Dot, ask their guardians to undertake community or charity volunteering in return for their accommodation. But Dawson says such schemes have mostly developed as a response to the expense of private renting. Crucially, it lowers people's expectations of what housing should do.

Floating homes: life on the water

In 2013, the London Assembly estimated that 10,000 people live on London's canals and rivers.[3] Holders of temporary mooring licences – which require each boat to move to a new spot every two weeks – rose from 626 in 2011 to 957 in 2013 in Paddington.[4] Those who can raise £15,000 to £20,000 can buy a houseboat with heating and basic facilities, and 50 per cent bank loans are available to some. Others rent boats for around £500 a month in London: a sum that only a few years ago might have paid for a rented flat. Permanent moorings are in high demand and cost around £5,500 per year in west London. According to 'Moor or Less', the 2013 report from the

London Assembly's environment committee, some mooring spots have waiting lists several years long.

Alexa (not her real name) was born in London. Throughout her twenties, she rented rooms in house-shares, which, she says, was 'hugely unsatisfactory'. Now in her forties, she has lived on boats for 20 years. She owns her boat but does not have a mooring license, temporary or permanent, so moves frequently to avoid being caught by inspectors. 'I refuse to allow anyone to romanticise boat life', she says. 'You have practical issues to deal with, like 25 kg bags of coal and toilets to empty.' Without a permanent address, it is hard for Alexa to register with a GP, to put herself on the electoral roll or to claim social security payments. She is healthy, but other boaters struggle to get the medical care they need, she says. 'Lots of people enjoy this life, but it's not easy', Alexa says.

Claire, another boater, works as a political advisor in the European Parliament. She says her decision to buy a boat for £35,000 was '90 per cent a response to high rent'. Living on her boat on the border of Essex, paying £160 a month in mooring fees, leaves her with disposable income after housing costs – something she never had as a private renter, when she paid £700 a month for a room in a shared flat. She had already familiarised herself with boat life by renting one a few years before she bought, but the final straw came when she experienced a no-fault eviction from her rented flat in Walthamstow in east London. 'In the last couple of years our landlord noticed what was happening to the property market, so evicted us and sold up', she says. She describes her boat as 'tiny', but sees this as a cost-effective solution to a much wider problem, and thinks the housing crisis is the effect of a political failure to intervene in the market.

'Affordable' housing and shared ownership

Shared ownership schemes were designed around 30 years ago as a way for low and middle income renters to buy homes, usually from housing associations. People buy a share of their home (usually between 25 and 75 per cent) and pay monthly rent on the rest, buying a bigger share if and when their earnings increase. But these schemes rarely offer a good deal; a 2012 study by Cambridge University found most owners were unable to increase their share and unable to sell their homes if they wanted to move on. Those who do sell very often do so for less than they originally paid.[5]

Shared ownership homes are typically flats on a 99-year lease, rather than a freehold, so residents also pay a service charge and ground rent to the freeholder: a cost which, when added to monthly rent and mortgage payments, can push the overall cost far out of the reach of people on average incomes. Other research from the University of York in 2015 found widespread confusion among part-owners and the housing associations who provide the schemes over who is responsible for repairs and maintenance.[6]

Francesca (not her real name) is a housing officer for a London housing association. She shows prospective tenants and part-owners around available accommodation, and deals with tenants' complaints. Like many housing associations, Francesca's provides rented accommodation for social tenants as well as shared-ownership schemes for part-owners, and facilities such as parking and green space and entrances are segregated according to tenure – even, she says, if tenants have physical disabilities. If a part-owner declines a car parking space (which comes at an extra cost), the housing association does not offer the space to a social tenant for fear the decision would become 'too complicated', she says.

For relatively well-off private renters desperate to escape the rent trap (half of those who take up shared-ownership schemes earn above £27,000 per year),[7] these schemes are a relief, but Francesca says she has noticed that some part-owners – and the companies who cater for them – cling to the idea that people should be categorised according to their type of tenure. Legally, politically and financially, private renters are now at the bottom of the pile, but an outdated sense that they are 'better' than social tenants prevails, Francesca says. At a recent viewing, a prospective social tenant waited for Francesca at the leaseholders' entrance by mistake – an entrance with a concierge desk and 'fancy lighting'. The door for social tenants was on the other side of the building and looks, she says, like a 'service entrance'. Francesca led them around to the entrance set aside for social tenants (a long walk), and they did not object, but she describes the experience as 'very embarrassing'.

Francesca says leaseholders represent between 10 and 20 per cent of the residents, but take up 80 per cent of her time. Vulnerable tenants, who need help to manage their home and keep on top of their finances, do not always get the help they need. When the housing association holds consultations on how to improve the area, leaseholders are more vociferous and wield more influence, she thinks. Some have demanded that funds be spent on installing CCTV rather than on communal play areas or gardening services, and Francesca believes this comes from a fear of social tenants. 'The people who lose out from these schemes are the tenants who need the most support', she says.

Dave and Kim rent their homes from, Camden Council, which has built a new mixed-tenure block called Chester Balmore. They are social tenants, and, like Francesca, have noticed a sense of segregation. Dave was rehoused here after the demolition of his council estate in Gospel Oak in 2011, while Kim lived in the block that existed on the current site before it was demolished for redevelopment. The new estate of 21 council flats and 23 leasehold flats looks pleasant: there are tree-lined streets next to a new playground with carved snakes. But, Dave says, it didn't take long for the relationship between the social tenants and leaseholders to deteriorate. Both say the housing officers employed by the council to manage the estate favour the leaseholders: complaints against tenants are regularly upheld whereas those against leaseholders go nowhere, they say. The leaseholders don't tend to interact with tenants, which means prejudice and myths are common. 'They think we are on benefits, that we don't pay rent or bills and that we are lucky to live here amongst them', says Kim.

In 2012, the Localism Act granted local authorities the power to keep the rents they collected from social tenants to use as they see fit, and some councils, such as Bristol and Norwich, have taken the chance to build new council housing. But local councils cannot build enough to house 11 million private renters; the Local Government Association estimates that under their current financial regime, councils could build only 10,000 homes a year nationally.[8] As an alternative, some councils have begun to consider entering the private rental market themselves. When Barking and Dagenham Council bought 144 homes from a private developer in September 2015 in order to let them out at 80 per cent of market rates (significantly higher than social rents), more than a thousand people registered an interest in the homes.[9]

Co-operative housing

Housing co-operatives provide around 1 per cent of housing stock in the UK. They are privately owned houses or collections of houses, but owned collectively by their members – who cannot profit individually. Some co-ops are 'fully mutual', providing housing to their members only and expecting them to actively participate in the management of the co-operative. Others are not, and do not require tenants to be members or to be involved at the same level.[10]

Alison Power has lived in the Ash Co-op in Cambridge for 13 years. It was built in the late 1970s using a grant from the Housing Corporation, a now defunct quango, and houses 75 people. Cambridge has some of the highest private rents in the UK, driven up by moves to make the city an 'economic powerhouse', bringing in high-profile tech companies employing high-earning professionals. Finding any type of housing in Cambridge has become extremely difficult, Alison says.

'I see more and more friends having to move out of Cambridge because they cannot afford to rent here', she says. One friend paid £850 a month for a small terraced house, but when they left the city they saw their house immediately advertised online for £1,200 a month. But the co-op's low rents, at £70 per week including bills, have allowed Alison to start her own business. Many of her fellow co-operative tenants are self-employed or work in creative industries, she says. Playing an active role in the management of their home is an important part of co-op life: Alison is part of the management committee, and has had responsibility for allocations, education and maintenance. Ash Co-op has plans to build new housing on some land currently owned by Cambridge Council.

John Fitzmaurice, director of Self-Help Housing, has set up housing co-operatives, housing associations and community land trusts over the last 30 years. He says radical changes in funding have damaged the alternative housing landscape: the amount of funding for smaller organisations has shrunk to almost nothing as the Homes and Community Agency (which replaced the Housing Corporation) has focused on larger housing associations and developers. Housing associations, once the vanguard of alternative housing in the 1970s, have become 'very corporate', he says, as the rules have been set to encourage them to act like profit-making businesses. The biggest associations are now national companies that own hundreds of thousands of homes: the 'G15' group of housing associations made a profit of £1 billion in 2014.[11] Ironically, many housing associations were set up because councils were seen as 'too big and faceless'. But, Fitzmaurice says, they have lost their original intentions.

Giroscope in Hull houses 29 people, charging them rents affordable to people on low incomes and housing benefit. It began in the 1980s when a group of activists pooled their money to buy a derelict house, then renovated it and let the rooms to raise money to buy the next one. Giroscope employs ex-offenders and the long-term unemployed to work on the renovation and management of the housing stock. Martin Newman, one of the Giroscope's founders, says they offer a much needed alternative to private landlords. 'We do not charge deposits, rent in advance, or admin fees. We maintain properties to a high standard. We encourage long-term tenancies and we charge fair and appropriate rents. We also house people who are often discriminated against in the private rented sector.'

Small housing organisations such as Giroscope, and Canopy and Latch in Leeds, call what they do 'self-help housing'. They want to revive the housing activism of the 1960s and 1970s by focusing on bringing empty homes back into use. As soon as a group buys a property – or, in some cases, is given one – they start fixing it up and letting it out. They also apply for funding from grant-making organisations including their local council. Latch has different rent levels for different sized houses, and uses its funds to discount rents for working tenants. The rent for a one-bed home is £161.58 a week, discounted down to £58 a week if necessary.

Jaime Risner began to create a housing co-op three years ago when he was a university student in Sheffield, and the first tenant moved into it in autumn 2015.[12] He and his fellow students were tired of the poor conditions and high rents that local private landlords offered, as well as the disconnection between students and local communities. They looked to the US, where student housing co-ops have existed for decades, providing housing for students and boosting community cohesion. They found a co-operative phone company to put up the initial funding and will repay them from the rental income. 'There's so much knowledge transfer that needs to happen', he says. 'It took us three years to get to this point.' He adds that being part of a housing co-op can help develop a more co-operative approach in other parts of life, too, like work.

The 'big moment', he says, will come when the mortgage is paid off, and co-op members can decide how to invest the rental income in other community projects. Some older housing co-ops have built up large reserves, but fail to invest the capital, so the point at which they've paid off their debts is pivotal. In the US, many 'socially conscious' businesses began their lives as housing co-ops. Sheffield is not the only city where students are looking to set up housing co-ops. One student co-op in Edinburgh now houses 106 students,[13] and there are plans to establish one in Birmingham, too.[14]

Globally, Sweden leads the way for co-operative housing, which makes up more than 20 per cent of the country's housing stock. In the 1920s and '30s, tenants set up the Swedish Co-operative Housing Association (HSB), which today owns 27,000 homes. Later, in the 1940s, trade unions set up another co-op, Riksbyggen, with state funding. Seven decades later, Riksbyggen has built a tenth of all housing in Sweden.[15] As soon as construction finishes on a building, Riksbyggen hands it over to a smaller co-op to manage.

FUCVAM in Uruguay is a federation with 500 housing co-ops as members, together housing 90,000 people. Members donate labour or materials towards the construction of their homes, equivalent to 15 per cent of the total cost. The other 85 per cent comes from a subsidised low-interest government loan, paid off over 20 years or more. The people who benefit from the co-ops are often the poorest in the community, who would otherwise struggle to afford decent housing.[16]

The growth of new co-op housing, especially for students, is exciting. But there is little funding available to scale these projects up. Central and local funding for community housing, once plentiful in the 1970s and '80s, has gone and is unlikely to be revived. While the private renters' movement in the UK is still emerging and lacks resources, UK trade unions have nearly 6 million members and huge financial and institutional power.[17] Were the unions to set up a primary building co-op, as in Sweden, co-operative housing could offer a viable escape from the rent trap.

Community land trusts

Gladstone Mews is a pleasant cul-de-sac in the Boscombe area of Bournemouth, in one of the most deprived areas of the South East. On the parallel road a sign for the local food bank says it's open four days a week. The entrance to the Mews is guarded by a small orchard of five trees, with plans afoot to plant a wildflower strip. On the other side is the old school house, a building owned by the local council. Having originally served as a community arts centre, it is now an 'enterprise space' for small businesses and a community centre. Further into the road are 11 homes built and designed to be permanently affordable: the first homes built by Bourne-mouth's community land trust.

Community land trusts (CLTs) started in the US in 1969 when civil rights activists founded New Communities Incorporated to provide 5,000 acres of farm land and leased housing.[18] 'It wasn't just enough to have rights. It was about power through owning land', says Catherine Hetherington, director of the UK Community Land Trust Network.

Community land trusts are non-profit organisations that own land. They build housing on the land, the trustees deciding for themselves whether it should be privately rented, owner-occupied, collectively owned or a combination of all three. Though a CLT is not a defined legal entity in itself, like a co-operative or a housing association, it must still meet legal requirements: it must benefit a specific community (for example, a town or village); people who live or work locally must have the opportunity to become members; and, crucially, the members must be the people who control the CLT.[19] According to the handbook published by the CLT Network, a steering group with as few as six people can start things off by setting out clear goals and a 'vision'. They then register as a company limited by guarantee (or, if they prefer, a charity or Community Interest Company), elect a board of directors or trustees, and start raising funds. When they've raised enough money, they can buy or acquire land and build housing on it. The community land trust acts as the steward of the homes and assets after they are built.

What keeps the homes permanently affordable is an 'asset lock' built into all CLTs, meaning the land can never be sold for profit. Instead, it could be transferred to another organisation with an asset lock, such as another charity. In the UK, CLT homes can be sold at no more than a third above the median income of the local area, so they help to preserve existing communities. There's no guarantee that individuals involved with a CLT will benefit personally from the new housing built, but many do – especially in urban areas. 'We are not building enough homes or enough of what people want in terms of affordability, quality and design', Hetherington says.

The UK's first CLT was founded in 1983. By 2010 there were 50 CLTs, and by 2015 there were 170 across the UK.[20] Unlike other new housing developments, the existing local community is in control of what gets built, Hetherington says. This is particularly useful in rural areas: in Cornwall, for example, the rate of newly built affordable housing has doubled since community land trusts began in 2006. This is partly because CLTs are allowed to build on otherwise restricted 'rural exception sites' – areas where second home owners buying holiday homes can outbid locals.

The Gladstone Mews homes in Bournemouth were all sold as shared-ownership homes, with the trust keeping a 35 per cent share and the freehold to ensure that the homes remain affordable. Tina Thompson from Bournemouth 2026, the charity that owns the CLT, says the homes were designed for families who were living in overcrowded council or housing association flats, some of which were already in shared ownership, but were too small to meet the needs of the families living in them. Urban projects like the East London CLT also focus on the 'intermediate' market, competing with shared-ownership housing being built by housing associations and councils.

But private renters looking for a quick and easy escape from the rent trap will not find it in a CLT, which takes years to develop. Some CLTs focus on fast development, building their housing through partnership with a housing association. This 'lite' version of the CLT means making compromises that could, in the long run, cause problems: as housing associations, they are now vulnerable to the current government's plans to expand the Right to Buy, which could force them to sell their assets into private hands.[21] Others that take longer to develop have so far retained control.

The attitude of local authorities towards CLTs varies, says Hetherington. Some, such as Cornwall, are very encouraging: Cornwall Council has set up a £4 million 'revolving loan fund' for CLT developments. Hetherington says this is a relatively easy way to generate the finance needed for development, as councils can borrow on more favourable terms than other bodies can. In Bournemouth, too, the council provided some of the start-up funding for the local CLT. With a solid income, they can employ staff rather than rely on volunteers.

The more the cost of land for development rises, particularly in urban areas like London, the harder it is for CLTs to raise the necessary funds to buy it. Tina Thompson is now looking for a second site in Bournemouth, but is finding it hard to compete with private developers, the council and housing associations. Hetherington says it's hard to encourage lenders to take on risk, especially during the early stages of a CLT. But the CLT Network have set up some grant funds to get CLTs off the ground using money from charitable trusts (including Esmée Fairbairn, Nationwide Foundation and Tudor Trust) to get their projects to the planning stage. 'Community land trusts need to be one part of the solution', Hetherington says, but she concedes they cannot solve the housing crisis on their own.

Short-term escape routes from the rent trap, such as property guardian schemes and houseboats, can only ever be temporary. Not just because they only suit those who are able to sacrifice legal rights and decent conditions in return for slightly lower rents, but because, as the housing crisis worsens, those rents too will rise. Housing co-operatives and community land trusts can grow, but not at the scale needed to house everyone who needs a secure, decent, affordable home. To do that, they would need huge investment from government, banks, or even, as was the case in Sweden, trade unions.

While the supply of – and political support for – social housing dwindles, and alternatives remain niche solutions, buy-to-let mortgages are booming. One in five homes is now owned by a private landlord,[22] and despite modest curbs introduced in 2015, buy-to-let is still going strong. With daily encouragement to see houses as capital assets rather than homes, Cameron's 'starter homes' plan, which will help those households on incomes of £50,000 (£77,000 in London) or more into homeownership, will turn first-time buyers into first-time landlords.[23] Increasing the number of people able to get a mortgage without increasing the supply of homes available to buy will push house prices up even further, locking out far more than it will let in. And the real winners of the race to build over green-belt land will be commercial developers, who refuse to build anything but the most profitable of housing. Profit paid for by the desperate.

A century after the Glasgow rent strikes, the UK's 11 million private renters are growing desperate. Private renters in Europe look on aghast, not quite believing that the fundamental rights they take for granted are denied to their British counterparts. But despite the best efforts of the landlord lobby, there are tiny glimmers of hope. No-fault eviction has been lightly restricted, and there are even plans on the table to ban it altogether in Scotland. Scotland and Wales already have mandatory national licensing, and many local authorities in England are adopting it. Candidates vying to become Mayor of London are calling for rent controls – an idea that would have been considered absurd a decade ago. National housing charities are getting through, and civil servants are tiring of the landlord lobby. Self-organised renters' groups are springing up everywhere.

'People base their level of satisfaction on what they feel is possible', said Alice in Chapter 7. It's time to look again at what that could be.

How to Take Your Landlord to Court

Dirghayu Patel

Since 2013, it has become much harder (though not impossible) to get legal aid for housing cases. So if you want to take your landlord to court, you might have to be a 'litigant in person' (LIP). This means doing it yourself.

This is a guide to using the civil courts to bring a claim against your landlord. Criminal cases use different courts, and criminal cases are handled by the police, the Crown Prosecution Service (CPS) or your council.

There are two parts to advocacy: written (preparing letters, witness statements and written arguments) and oral (presenting your case in court).

Written advocacy

Too often, people overlook the written side to advocacy, but it is important to get it right. It starts with writing a letter to your landlord. You need to do this as soon as possible. You will need to show that you have given your landlord the chance to respond, and to accept or deny liability. If your landlord does not reply, or denies liability, you can't be criticised for bringing your case to court and you will be in a stronger position to recoup your court costs if you win. A good letter should:

(a) be concise

(b) set out the factual and legal basis of the claim

(c) give a deadline for them to reply

(d) set out any disclosure that is required (i.e., any document that the landlord has which may support your case)

Your landlord might choose to settle the matter at this stage. If s/he doesn't, the next task is to draft your case. This involves completing two key documents: the claim form and the 'particulars of claim'. These documents are important because they allow you to tell the court and your landlord (a) why you are doing this and (b) what you want to get.

'Particulars of claims' should outline the legal and factual elements of your claim. In most housing cases the legal elements are:

1. The existence of a duty. The duty could be contractual, for example, the duty to allow quiet enjoyment of your home. This is an implied term of any tenancy agreement, even if it doesn't say it in your contract. If you have been illegally evicted, your landlord has breached his duty to allow you quiet enjoyment of your home. In the 'particulars of claim', you should identify the people involved in the tenancy agreement (give the names of the landlord and tenants), give the dates of your tenancy, and outline the terms of the tenancy agreement. Remember, as long as you've got proof of the rent you have paid

(for example, from your bank statement) then it doesn't matter if you don't have a written tenancy agreement, because the same terms and conditions apply.

Alternatively, the duty could be based on common law tort (for example, failure to keep the property in good repair resulting in personal injury to occupiers who are not tenants) or a statutory tort (for example, failure to pay a deposit into an approved scheme, or failure to provide prescribed information such as a gas safety certificate).

2. The breach of the duty. For example, if the case is about disrepair, the breach would be the landlord's failure to carry out the repairs within a reasonable time. Here you should explain how the breach happened. You should describe the disrepair, give the dates of when you told your landlord about it, and show that they did not fix it within a reasonable period of time.

3. The existence of loss. This is where you should show you have lost out in some way. In cases about breach of contract it is usually the 'loss of benefit expected in tenancy', meaning you lost the comfort or enjoyment of your home.

The factual basis of the claim must include all three things set out above. Normally, you should not include evidence in this part.

You will need to estimate the value of your case. This affects how your case is handled by the court. It will also affect the court fee you will need to pay.*

* http://hmctsformfinder.justice.gov.uk/courtfinder/forms/ex050-eng.pdf

Value of your claim	Court issued claim	Filed via SDT/MCOL*
£0 – £300	£35.00	£25.00
£301 – £500	£50.00	£35.00
£501 – £1,000	£70.00	£60.00
£1,001 – £1,500	£80.00	£70.00
£1,501 – £3,000	£115.00	£105.00
£3,001 – £5,000	£205.00	£185.00
£5,001 – £10,000	£455.00	£410.00
£10,000 – £15,000	5% of the claim	4.5% of the claim
£15,000 – £50,000	5% of the claim	4.5% of the claim
£50,000 – £100,000	5% of the claim	4.5% of the claim
£100,000 – £150,000	5% of the claim	N/A
£150,001 – £200,000	5% of the claim	N/A
£200,001 or more	£10,000.00	N/A

* Maximum amount for Secure Data Transfer (SDT) or Money Claim OnLine (MCOL) £99,999.99

People receiving any of the following benefits can claim these fees back:

- Income-based Job Seekers' Allowance
- Income-based Employment Support Allowance
- Income Support
- Universal Credit – with gross annual earnings of less than £6,000
- State Pension – Guarantee Credit
- Scottish Civil Legal Aid

People can also claim their fees back depending on their earnings and family size. The income thresholds are:

Gross monthly income with:	Single	Couple
No children	£1,085.00	£1,245.00
One child	£1,330.00	£1,490.00
Two children	£1,575.00	£1,735.00

Plus £245 for each additional child (http://hmctsformfinder. justice.gov.uk/courtfinder/forms/ex160a-eng.pdf).

Even people earning significantly more can claim part of their fees back. The income thresholds are:

Gross monthly income with:	Single	Couple
No children	£5,085.00	£5,245.00
One child	£5,330.00	£5,490.00
Two children	£5,575.00	£5,735.00

Plus £245 for each additional child (http://hmctsformfinder. justice.gov.uk/courtfinder/forms/ex160a-eng.pdf).

To find the most recent guidance (at time of writing this is the 'Civil and Family Court Fees' published on 6 April 2015) go to the Ministry of Justice website: https://www.justice.gov. uk/courts/fees.

The next part of written advocacy deals with evidence. This is where you should prepare a witness statement. The 'burden of proof' is on you. This means it is up to you to prove that what you are saying is true; it is not up to your landlord to prove it is false. Lots of people think that if you haven't got evidence, your case will automatically fail. But this is not true. The best evidence can be your own testimony, as long as it is credible and detailed.

In your witness statement, you should give evidence that backs up what you are saying. For example, if you are pursuing a claim for damages for disrepair, you can set out the existence of your tenancy agreement, the history of the disrepair, how the landlord was told about it, what their response was and what the effect of their failure to fix it was (i.e., what you or other people in your house lost as a result).

In a tenancy deposit case, you can set out when the deposit was paid, how it was paid and whether you received the information about which deposit protection scheme it was paid into. Any documents you have should be mentioned here – for example, a letter or email to the landlord informing him of disrepair.

There are 'civil procedure rules' about witness statements, so it's important to get all the details right. The most important requirement is that there is a 'statement of truth' which means a statement confirming your belief that the facts you have given are correct, with your signature on it. It should also have a heading containing your name and your landlord's, and it should be double line spaced with page numbers.

Before you prepare your witness statement, the court expects each party (i.e., you and your landlord) to 'make disclosure'. This is where you have to tell your landlord about all the documents you have that are relevant, and they have to do the same. Getting disclosure from your landlord will help you prepare your witness statement.

If your landlord won't give disclosure, then you can win automatically by applying to have them struck out for not following court instructions. To obtain this kind of order, known as an 'unless order', you need to make an application to the court on form N244. In the application you should say what you want the court to do (i.e., make an unless order) and why (i.e., non-compliance with court directions).

Having a well-drafted 'particulars of claim' and a detailed witness statement will give you a good advantage as you approach the trial. In lots of civil cases, the landlord settles the case by offering you money, to end it there and avoid the cost of a trial. If he doesn't do this, or if you do not want to 'settle', you should prepare for the final hearing.

Write out a skeleton argument summarising the arguments you plan to make and what decision you think the court should make. Keep it short. A skeleton argument should have:

1. An introduction setting out the relevant legal and factual issues and what your case will be. For example: 'This is to claim damages against the defendant for his failure to comply with tenancy deposit provisions set out in the Housing Act 2004 as amended by the Localism Act 2011.'
2. A chronology: what happened, with all dates.
3. A summary of the relevant legal provisions.
4. Your submissions, applying the facts to the law to result in your conclusion. For example: 'The defendant is liable to pay damages plus return the deposit for his failure to protect the deposit in an approved scheme.'

A skeleton argument helps you to prepare for the trial, and it also helps the judge at the trial.

Oral advocacy

Presenting your case at the final hearing might be daunting, but if you have prepared well you should not be afraid.

Most people get their ideas about what court is like from TV dramas, but these are not realistic. Besides, you will be using a civil court rather than a criminal one. Unlike criminal trials, civil hearings usually don't have a jury. The trial will be conducted by a district judge. Being dramatic or trying to 'perform' to the court in the style of a TV drama will usually work against you. Stick to clear and simple language that addresses all the relevant legal and factual issues in the case.

It is likely that your landlord will be represented by a legally qualified person. If that person is a solicitor, there are rules about how they should behave. For example, the Law Society has written a code for solicitors who are opposed by a litigant in person (LIP).[1] The code says they should not take advantage of you by:

- using bullying and unjustifiable threats
- using misleading or deceitful behaviour
- claiming what cannot be properly claimed
- demanding what cannot properly be demanded

If your landlord's solicitor has broken the code, you should draw it to the judge's attention as well as informing the Solicitors Regulation Authority.

As the claimant, you will have to go first. This starts with an opening speech outlining the relevant legal and factual issues. This should include the reasons why you are bringing the case and the reasons why your landlord is defending it.

Once the opening speeches are over, the judge will ask for your evidence. There are three stages to the presentation of evidence. The first stage is 'examination in chief' where you call your witness. Unlike in criminal trials, your witness statement (which you have already prepared) stands as evidence. So all that happens is that you get asked whether your witness statement is true.

The second stage is cross-examination. This is your chance to challenge the evidence that your landlord has given. Do this by asking 'closed' questions that can only be answered yes or no. For example, if you paid your deposit in cash and your landlord is saying that he did not receive it from you, you could show that you withdrew the money from your bank account on the day your tenancy started. Your questioning could go like this:

Is it not correct that on 1 April 2012, a tenancy agreement was entered into?

Yes.

Is it not correct that the rental agreement states that the monthly rent is £400?

Yes.

Is it not correct that the rent must be paid a month in advance?

Yes.

Is it not correct that on 1 April 2012 (check the date on your bank statements), a sum of £800 was withdrawn from my account?

Yes.

Is it not correct that the sum was withdrawn to pay you the first month's rent and a deposit?

No.

In the exchange above, the landlord has not agreed with your analysis about the payment of the deposit. You cannot expect your landlord to cave in easily the way people do in TV court dramas. But the answers he gives are helpful because when making your closing speech you can comment on the fact that money had been withdrawn to pay one month's rent in advance. In this case, you would argue that the extra amount, which is equivalent to another month's rent, could only be for the purposes of a deposit and that therefore it is more likely than not that a deposit was paid.

The final part of witness evidence is re-examination. This is your chance to rebuild the credibility of your witness after your opponent has cross-examined them. You might be the only witness in your case, so it would be technically impossible for you to re-examine yourself. The judge will modify the way the case is presented to take this into account.

Once the evidence has been given, you will have the chance to make a closing speech. In the closing speech, you can comment on the evidence that the court has heard, including the evidence that you have heard in cross-examination.

After the closing speeches have been given, the district judge will make a decision. Normally the judgment is given immediately after the closing speeches, but if the trial has been very long there could be a delay. If this happens, you will need to come back to hear the decision. When the judge gives the judgment, keep careful notes. This will help you if you need to appeal afterwards.

If the decision goes against you, you can ask for permission to appeal. If you want to appeal, you must appeal to a circuit judge rather than a district judge. If the judge refuses you permission to appeal, you can still make a written application. This needs to be handed in within 21 days.

Notes

Chapter One

1. When contacted for comment on this incident, a Denfields spokesperson said she was satisfied with the conduct of the Denfields employee and that it 'wasn't worth getting into the nitty-gritty details'. We also contacted the landlord and gave him the right to reply – an offer he declined.
2. www.gov.uk/government/uploads/system/uploads/attachment_data/file/406740/English_Housing_Survey_Headline_Report_2013-14.pdf
3. http://england.shelter.org.uk/__data/assets/pdf_file/0007/1166956/Making_renting_fit_for_families_FINAL.pdf
4. LSE, 'Towards a sustainable private rented sector: The lessons from other countries', 2011, available at http://eprints.lse.ac.uk/56070
5. www.rla.org.uk/landlord/lobbying/docs/Longer_Tenancies_Consultation.pdf

Chapter Two

1. www.bbc.co.uk/news/uk-england-london-24372509
2. Shelter housing databank, accessed September 2015.
3. Figures accurate as at September 2015, using Hackney Council's benefits claim calculator, based on a monthly rent of between £1,104 and £2,000.
4. For further explanation, see www.theguardian.com/housing-network/2012/oct/26/council-homelessness-rules-housing-policy
5. Later that year, in December 2013, a further £4 million of central government funds was divided up between 23 councils to 'tackle rogue landlords', though licensing was not a specific requirement.

6. See the Appendix for a tenant's guide to taking a landlord to court.
7. http://nearlylegal.co.uk/2008/06/illegal-eviction-and-disrepair-damages/ and http://nearlylegal.co.uk/2015/01/unlawful-eviction-harassment-quantum-update/
8. www.landlordaction.co.uk/site.php/tenant/information/why_you_need_us_for_step_1
9. www.thestar.co.uk/news/local/sheffield-landlord-locked-up-after-throwing-tenant-on-street-1-4979570
10. www.landlordlawblog.co.uk/2010/07/21/unlawful-eviction-case---the-police-finally-brought-to-account

Chapter Three

1. www.theguardian.com/money/2014/jan/16/rents-rise-tenants-outstrip-supply
2. www.gov.uk/government/publications/private-rental-market-statistics-england-only/release-notes-10-june-2014.
3. www.theguardian.com/money/2014/jan/16/rents-rise-tenants-outstrip-supply
4. www.ons.gov.uk/ons/rel/hpi/index-of-private-housing-rental-prices/historical-series/iphrp-article.html#tab-What-is-the-Index-of-Private-Housing-Rental-Prices
5. http://england.shelter.org.uk/__data/assets/pdf_file/0007/624391/Rent_trap_v4.pdf
6. www.housing.org.uk/media/blog/private-renters-in-uk-pay-double-the-european-average/
7. www.cityam.com/215744/uk-house-price-growth-means-regional-rents-are-now-rising-faster-london
8. www.theguardian.com/money/2015/apr/10/bristol-tenants-plan-demo-letting-agents-rent-rise
9. www.theguardian.com/money/2015/apr/10/bristol-tenants-plan-demo-letting-agents-rent-rise
10. ONS, House Price Index, December 2014, Tables 34 and 38.
11. www.thisismoney.co.uk/money/mortgageshome/article-2918348/House-deposits-rise-71-000-tougher-lending-rules-stamp-duty-reforms-push-sums-laid-buyers-higher.html

12. www.yumpu.com/en/document/view/34837314/1e75imu
13. www.cityam.com/1409101890/letting-agents-raise-rents-get-around-ban-fees
14. http://england.shelter.org.uk/__data/assets/pdf_file/0010/834832/6636_Scottish_letting_fees_report_v9.pdf
15. www.bbc.co.uk/news/uk-scotland-19002304
16. www.bbc.co.uk/news/uk-22095712
17. http://prsupdate.co.uk/2013/05/tenancy-deposit-scheme
18. www.independent.co.uk/news/uk/politics/almost-nobody-in-the-uk-is-opposed-to-rent-controls-for-housing-9955679.html
19. www.civitas.org.uk/pdf/thefuturcofprivaterenting
20. www.france24.com/en/20150801-rent-control-law-paris-france-effect-regulations
21. www.theguardian.com/world/2015/jun/01/rent-cap-legislation-in-force-berlin-germany
22. http://en.myeurop.info/2012/06/06/rent-control-a-success-across-northern-europe-5530
23. www.lse.ac.uk/geographyAndEnvironment/research/london/pdf/Rent-Stabilisation-report-2014.pdf
24. http://venezuelanalysis.com/news/7509
25. http://www.cchpr.landecon.cam.ac.uk/Projects/Start-Year/2015/The-effects-of-rent-controls-on-supply-and-markets
26. http://www.theguardian.com/money/2015/jul/06/shelter-blunt-rent-cap-harm-tenants-unregulated-properties
27. www.jrf.org.uk/media-centre/soaring-rent-nearly-6million-private-renters-poverty-2040-6591
28. www.theguardian.com/housing-network/2014/nov/26/-sp-private-renters-living-in-poverty
29. www.civitas.org.uk/pdf/thefutureofprivaterenting
30. www.theguardian.com/society/2015/mar/14/housing-benefit-coalition-people-claiming
31. www.insidehousing.co.uk/nearly-11bn-housing-benefit-paid-to-private-landlords-by-2019/7003417.article
32. http://blog.shelter.org.uk/2015/07/budget-2015-unpicking-the-unravelling-of-housing-benefit

33. www.gov.uk/government/uploads/system/uploads/attachment_data/file/329902/rr874-lha-impact-of-recent-reforms-summary.pdf
34. www.bbc.co.uk/news/uk-politics-11637928
35. www.bbc.co.uk/news/uk-england-london-11979147
36. www.crisis.org.uk/data/files/publications/Crisis%20briefing%20on%20the%20Shared%20Accommodation%20Rate.pdf
37. www.londonspovertyprofile.org.uk/indicators/topics/receiving-non-work-benefits/national-benefit-caps
38. www.independent.co.uk/news/uk/politics/budget-2015-benefits-cap-to-be-reduced-to-20000-for-families-outside-london-10367590.html
39. www.insidehousing.co.uk/dwp-housing-benefit-will-be-sanctioned/7002330.article?adfesuccess=1
40. www.crisis.org.uk/data/files/publications/Crisis%20Briefing%20-%20Housing%20Benefit%20cuts.pdf

Chapter Four

1. http://england.shelter.org.uk/__data/assets/pdf_file/0003/1039530/FINAL_SAFE_AND_DECENT_HOMES_REPORT-_USE_FOR_LAUNCH.pdf
2. www.citymetric.com/horizons/6-reasons-why-private-renting-sucks-778
3. www.natcen.ac.uk/our-research/research/health,-mental-health-and-housing-conditions-in-england
4. http://england.shelter.org.uk/__data/assets/pdf_file/0009/781587/Final_copy_of_Shelters_response_to_the_Government_Review_into_poor_conditions.pdf
5. www.essex.ac.uk/hhs/documents/research/clacton-bedsit-report.pdf
6. www.bbc.co.uk/news/uk-27940701
7. www.channel4.com/news/sofa-surfing-hidden-homeless-britain-youth-benefits

8. www.civitas.org.uk/pdf/thefutureofprivaterenting; http://
   england.shelter.org.uk/__data/assets/pdf_file/0020/574202/
   LHA_affordability_final.pdf
9. www.thebureauinvestigates.com/2013/06/08/westminster-hit-
   by-soaring-costs-as-it-struggles-to-cope-with-homeless-
   epidemic
10. www.crisis.org.uk/data/files/publications/MysteryShopping_
    Report_FINAL_web.pdf
11. www.insidehousing.co.uk/homelessness-services-experience-
    cuts-in-funding/7008621.article
12. http://m.insidehousing.co.uk/councils-spend-18m-on-
    sweeteners-for-private-landlords/7009703.article
13. www.homeless.org.uk/connect/blogs/2014/oct/06/bridging-
    gap-between-private-landlords-and-homelessness-services
14. www.cih.org/news-article/display/vpathDCR/templatedata/
    cih/news-article/data/Use_autumn_statement_to_support_
    private_tenants_at_risk_of_becoming_homeless_says_CIH
15. Welsh Local Government Association, 'Social Lettings Agencies
    in Wales', 2013. http://www.wlga.gov.uk/report-social-lettings-
    agencies-in-wales

Chapter Five

1. www.theguardian.com/politics/2015/may/26/landlords-14bn-
   tax-breaks-buy-to-let-expansion-mortgage-interest
2. www.independent.co.uk/news/uk/politics/advice-encouraging-
   landlords-to-stalk-potential-tenants-withdrawn-10124275.html?
   origin=internalSearch
3. www.theguardian.com/money/2015/aug/06/average-house-
   price-rises-times-local-salary-england-wales
4. http://news.rla.org.uk/rla-meeting-with-housing-minister
5. www.mancunianmatters.co.uk/content/270473292-landlord-
   group-want-more-support-councils-not-laws-help-manchester-
   tenants

6. www.theargus.co.uk/news/12942652.Political_posturing_is_
failing_private_tenants_in_Brighton___Hove__Opinion_by_
Alan_Ward

7. www.southportreporter.com/705/705-8.shtml#axzz3k1pdWpxi

8. See Figure 1 on page 10.

9. www.guardian-series.co.uk/news/wfnews/13315936.Renters_
in_Walthamstow_pay_average_of___484_in_letting_fees__
research_reveals

Chapter Six

1. Joseph Melling, *Rent Strikes*, Polygon Books, 1983, p. 94.

2. www.theguardian.com/money/2015/jul/16/tenants-in-
england-spend-half-their-pay-on-rent

3. These amounts were calculated using the National Archives
currency calculator: www.nationalarchives.gov.uk/currency

4. The meeting notes and newspaper articles were provided by
Peabody, who still provide social housing.

5. www.parliament.uk/about/living-heritage/transformingsociety/
towncountry/towns/overview/towns

6. www.legislation.gov.uk/ukpga/Vict/48-49/72/contents

7. Lynsey Hanley, *Estates: An Intimate History*, Granta, 2007, p. 56.

8. Hanley, *Estates*, p. 55.

9. http://sites.scran.ac.uk/redclyde/redclyde/docs/rcpeomary
barbour.htm

10. Melling, *Rent Strikes*, p. 67.

11. www.bbc.co.uk/programmes/p01sgk4m

12. Melling, *Rent Strikes*, p. 94.

13. http://sites.scran.ac.uk/redclyde/redclyde/rc185.htm

14. Melling, *Rent Strikes*, p. 95.

15. Melling, *Rent Strikes*, p. 92.

16. www.british-history.ac.uk/vch/essex/vol5/pp267-281

17. www.parliament.uk/about/living-heritage/transformingsociety/
towncountry/towns/overview/councilhousing

18. http://dro.dur.ac.uk/9820/1/9820.pdf

19. http://dro.dur.ac.uk/9820/1/9820.pdf

20. Nicholas Timmins, *The Five Giants: A Biography of the Welfare State*, HarperCollins, 2001, quoted in Hayley, *Estates*, p. 79.

21. http://humanities.exeter.ac.uk/media/universityofexeter/ collegeofhumanities/history/exhistoria/volume4/Webber-Squatters_movement.pdf

22. http://humanities.exeter.ac.uk/media/universityofexeter/ collegeofhumanities/history/exhistoria/volume4/Webber-Squatters_movement.pdf

23. Hanley, *Estates*, p. 90.

24. Hanley, *Estates*, p. 28.

25. Hanley, *Estates*, p. 97.

26. www.independent.co.uk/news/people/obituary-t-dan-smith-1487528.html

27. Councils had been able to sell off housing since 1936, with approval from the relevant government minister.

28. www.bbc.co.uk/news/uk-14380936

29. www.theguardian.com/housing-network/2013/apr/17/ margaret-thatcher-legacy-housing-crisis

30. www.mirror.co.uk/news/uk-news/right-to-buy-housing-shame-third-ex-council-1743338

31. https://fullfact.org/factchecks/council_house_building_ margaret_thatcher_labour_government-29270

32. www.civitas.org.uk/pdf/thefutureofprivaterenting

33. www.thesundaytimes.co.uk/sto/comment/regulars/archive/ article788167.ece

34. www.politicsresources.net/area/uk/man/lab66.htm

35. www.legislation.gov.uk/ukpga/1977/43

36. www.theguardian.com/law/2012/oct/30/london-rent-assessment-panel

37. www.civitas.org.uk/pdf/thefutureofprivaterenting

38. http://hansard.millbanksystems.com/commons/1988/ may/09/private-rented-housing#S6CV0133P0_19880509_ HOC_211

39. www.telegraph.co.uk/finance/personalfinance/investing/buy-to-let/11591986/Mortgage-rate-rise-would-make-buy-to-let-unviable-in-7-out-of-10-regions.html

Chapter Seven

1. www.theguardian.com/money/2012/feb/03/why-quite-buy-to-let
2. www.theguardian.com/money/2012/mar/09/tenants-landlords-grievances-online
3. www.bankofengland.co.uk/publications/Pages/fsr/2015/jul.aspx
4. www.theguardian.com/business/2015/apr/05/uk-pensioners-ready-to-jump-queue-for-property-osborne-revolution?CMP=share_btn_tw
5. www.theguardian.com/money/2015/jul/22/pwc-report-generation-rent-to-grow-over-next-decade
6. www.hertfordshiremercury.co.uk/Wareside-tax-evader-sentenced/story-21980733-detail/story.html
7. www.theguardian.com/politics/2015/may/26/landlords-14bn-tax-breaks-buy-to-let-expansion-mortgage-interest
8. www.theguardian.com/money/2014/mar/15/landlords-hmrc-undeclared-lettings-income-tax
9. www.telegraph.co.uk/finance/personalfinance/10999633/HMRC-turns-up-heat-on-landlords.html
10. www.landlordzone.co.uk/forums/showthread.php?54995-deposit-companies-grassing-landlords-up-to-HMRC
11. www.theguardian.com/business/2015/dec/27/landlords-launch-legal-challenge-against-george-osborne-tax-relief-changes

Chapter Eight

1. www.theguardian.com/money/2010/jan/10/property-guardian-schemes
2. https://propertyguardianresearch.wordpress.com/2014/08/20/property-guardians-in-the-uk-recent-developments-aug-2014
3. www.independent.co.uk/property/10000-people-living-on-boats-in-london-8967106.html

4. https://www.london.gov.uk/about-us/london-assembly/london-assembly-publications/moor-or-less-moorings-london%E2%80%99s-waterways
5. www.cam.ac.uk/research/news/a-problem-shared
6. www.theguardian.com/housing-network/2015/jul/03/shared-ownership-buyers-frustrated-charges
7. www.housing.org.uk/resource-library/browse/shared-ownership-meeting-aspiration
8. www.local.gov.uk/media-releases/-/journal_content/56/10180/5730845/NEWS
9. www.residentiallandlord.co.uk/council-enters-private-rental-sector
10. www.theguardian.com/society/2013/dec/01/woman-lambeth-council-home-faces-eviction
11. www.insidehousing.co.uk/londons-biggest-landlords-record-1bn-surplus/7004629.article
12. www.theguardian.com/money/2015/sep/07/student-co-ops-tackle-accommodation-costs-rent-property
13. www.students.coop/our-network/edinburgh-student-housing-co-operative
14. www.theguardian.com/sustainable-business/birmingham-students-housing-cooperative-exploitative-landlords
15. www.nabco.ie/_fileupload/Profiles%20of%20a%20movement.pdf
16. www.worldhabitatawards.org/winners-and-finalists/project-details.cfm?lang=00&theProjectID=9DC73800-15C5-F4C0-99F350F027EC172E
17. www.gov.uk/government/uploads/system/uploads/attachment_data/file/431564/Trade_Union_Membership_Statistics_2014.pdf
18. http://communitylandtrust.org/wp-content/uploads/2015/02/Origins-Evolution-CLT-byJohnDavis.pdf
19. www.carnegieuktrust.org.uk/getattachment/36205120-cb79-4fbc-847a-cb07f7830f1e/Community-Land-Trust-Handbook.aspx
20. www.communitylandtrusts.org.uk/what-is-a-clt/about-clts

21. www.communitylandtrusts.org.uk/about-the-network/our-campaigns
22. www.telegraph.co.uk/finance/personalfinance/investing/buy-to-let/11179073/Buy-to-let-boom-one-in-five-homes-now-owned-by-landlords.html
23. www.independent.co.uk/news/uk/politics/david-cameron-s-solution-to-the-housing-crisis-only-affordable-to-those-who-earn-more-than-50000-a6684246.html

Appendix

1. Law Society Practice Note 19.04.13, to be found at: www.lawsociety.org.uk/advice/practicenotes/litigants-in-person

Index

BEING RED

A Politics for the Future

by Ken Livingstone

**Suddenly the Labour Party is interesting again.
But how can it win back the popular vote and govern?**

With honesty and his trademark humour, there are few
better placed than Ken Livingstone to serve up an insider's
account of the Party and its future at a pivotal moment.

Taking us from the self-proclaimed 'radical socialism' of
the Greater London Council, through his two terms as
Mayor of London and his 2012 candidacy against Boris
Johnson, Ken Livingstone recounts his many battles
against privatisation, pollution and Tory politicians.

Being Red offers a practical path to the future.

Available now from Pluto Press
and the Left Book Club.

www.plutobooks.com
www.leftbookclub.com

SYRIZA
Inside the Labyrinth

by Kevin Ovenden

with a Foreword by Paul Mason

'A fascinating, humane, caustic analysis of
Greece and the rebirth of its left –
an inspiration for progressives everywhere'

Zoe Williams, the *Guardian*

'Mesmerising ... Ovenden cuts through
stereotypes and ignorance to tell the
story of the Greek resistance'

Paul Mason

Available now from Pluto Press and the Left Book Club.

www.plutobooks.com
www.leftbookclub.com